Risk Management in Outdoor and Adventure Programs

Scenarios of Accidents, Incidents, and Misadventures

Risk Management in Outdoor and Adventure Programs

Scenarios of Accidents, Incidents, and Misadventures

Aram Attarian

Human Kinetics

Library of Congress Cataloging-in-Publication Data

Attarian, Aram.
  Risk management in outdoor and adventure programs : scenarios of accidents, incidents, and misadventures / Aram Attarian.
     p. cm.
  Includes bibliographical references.
  ISBN 978-1-4504-0471-6 (soft cover) -- ISBN 1-4504-0471-5 (soft cover)
  1. Outdoor education. 2. Adventure education. 3. Risk management. I. Title.
  LB1047.A77 2012
  371.3'84--dc23

                                    2011048994

ISBN-10: 1-4504-0471-5 (print)
ISBN-13: 978-1-4504-0471-6 (print)

This publication is written and published to provide accurate and authoritative information relevant to the subject matter presented. It is published and sold with the understanding that the author and publisher are not engaged in rendering legal, medical, or other professional services by reason of their authorship or publication of this work. If medical or other expert assistance is required, the services of a competent professional person should be sought.

The web addresses cited in this text were current as of January 2012, unless otherwise noted.

Acquisitions Editor: Gayle Kassing, PhD; **Developmental Editor:** Ragen E. Sanner; **Assistant Editor:** Anne Rumery; **Copyeditor:** Patsy Fortney; **Permissions Manager:** Dalene Reeder; **Graphic Designer:** Joe Buck; **Graphic Artist:** Kathleen Boudreau-Fuoss; **Cover Designer:** Keith Blomberg; **Photographer (cover):** Courtesy of Aram Attarian; **Photographer (interior):** Photos on pages 1 and 65 courtesy of Aram Attarian; photo on page 25, Valeriy Pistryy/fotolia.com; photo on page 115, Vlad Turchenko/fotolia.com; all others © Human Kinetics, unless otherwise noted; **Art Manager:** Kelly Hendren; **Associate Art Manager:** Alan L. Wilborn; **Illustrations:** © Human Kinetics; **Printer:** United Graphics

Printed in the United States of America   10 9 8 7 6 5 4 3 2 1

The paper in this book is certified under a sustainable forestry program.

Human Kinetics
Website: www.HumanKinetics.com

United States: Human Kinetics
P.O. Box 5076
Champaign, IL 61825-5076
800-747-4457
e-mail: humank@hkusa.com

Canada: Human Kinetics
475 Devonshire Road Unit 100
Windsor, ON N8Y 2L5
800-465-7301 (in Canada only)
e-mail: info@hkcanada.com

Europe: Human Kinetics
107 Bradford Road, Stanningley
Leeds LS28 6AT, United Kingdom
+44 (0) 113 255 5665
e-mail: hk@hkeurope.com

Australia: Human Kinetics
57A Price Avenue
Lower Mitcham, South Australia 5062
08 8372 0999
e-mail: info@hkaustralia.com

New Zealand: Human Kinetics
P.O. Box 80
Torrens Park, South Australia 5062
0800 222 062
e-mail: info@hknewzealand.com

E5328

Contents

Scenario Finder

Chapter 5 Equipment

Chapter 6 Transportation

Preface

I've been involved in the outdoor adventure industry for more than 35 years. During this time I have had the opportunity to travel, meet people, experience storm and sorrow, see beautiful sunrises and sunsets, and change people's lives. In my formative years I took risks, had my share of injuries, and even had a brush with death. Needless to say, I learned a lot from these experiences!

Over the years I have become captivated by the accidents, incidents, and misadventures of others. By *captivated*, I mean that I have found some value, some lesson to be learned, in reading and hearing about others' misadventures. Some years ago I began collecting accident, incident, and misadventure reports primarily from personal and peer experiences, newspapers, outdoor program accident reports, and other resources including *Accidents in North American Mountaineering, River Safety Reports,* and the U.S. National Park Service's *Morning Report.* I started sharing my favorites with students and outdoor program instructors by way of introducing or reinforcing the key concepts of risk management, program planning, decision making, and problem solving.

Using scenarios of accidents, incidents, and misadventures as a teaching tool usually involves examining a single event or a series of related events in a systematic way. This helps students determine why the event happened and what might be done in the future to prevent it from happening again.

The use of scenarios as a training and teaching aid can also help students identify the human and environmental factors that cause accidents, increase their awareness of such factors, reinforce leadership, judgment, and decision-making skills, and establish a questioning attitude toward safety. The scenarios in this book and the questions that follow them are intended to place the reader into the role and mind-set of an outdoor leader or guide, basically asking, What would you do? As such, this book is intended to improve students' problem-solving skills, and to provide the opportunity to reflect on hazardous situations without having to live through them!

This book is an invaluable outdoor leadership training resource for college students training to be professional outdoor leaders. It will also benefit practicing outdoor leaders, guides, program administrators, and other professionals who integrate adventure activities into their classrooms, conduct staff trainings, or offer in-service programs.

This book can also be used as a supplemental resource in courses on risk management and outdoor adventure, or as a stand-alone resource. In lieu of a detailed discussion of the fundamentals of risk management, a number of risk management models and concepts are presented in the opening chapters as tools for readers to use when addressing the questions at the end of each scenario.

In all scenarios the names of the staff members, participants, programs, dates, and locations have been changed to ensure confidentiality. In some scenarios information has been added, changed, or deleted to make them more meaningful. Following each narrative is a set of discussion questions, some of which may require further investigation. Each scenario has the potential to open doorways for discussion and, in some cases, action. Trainers, educators, and other professionals are encouraged to modify the scenarios and add their own questions to make them more meaningful to their own programs, students, and teaching styles.

Chapter 1

Introduction
to Risk Management

Administrators, instructors, and professional guides working in adventure-based programs or organizations face critical decisions in their efforts to keep their participants safe from the dangers associated with risk-related activities. **Risk** is an essential element in the conduct of any guided or adventure program. The challenge for a guide or instructor is to strike a balance between real and perceived risk when delivering a course or program. Too little risk results in bored participants, whereas too much risk can be dangerous.

Taking appropriate risk management actions can reduce real risks while keeping perceived risks high. Managing risk in organized and guided adventure programs can reduce the probability and severity of accidents and injuries and minimize liability exposure for the organization and its employees. To minimize risk, program providers exert significant effort to address risk factors. A **risk factor** is something that increases the chances of a negative event occurring. Many of the misadventures that occur in guided and outdoor adventure programs are the result of inherent risks. **Inherent risks** are risks that cannot be eliminated without changing the nature of the activity.

To manage risks and enhance **safety**, program directors should establish a set of safety objectives while accepting the fact that mistakes can and will happen. Implementing backup systems, empowering employees to be responsible for safety, and analyzing and stressing the importance of accident and near-miss reporting should also be priorities for managing risk (Sagan, 1995).

Chapters 3 through 6 present scenarios in the following categories:

- Staff and participants—Chapter 3 addresses programs' workforce (instructors, guides, logisticians, administrators) and the people they serve (customers and clients).
- Environment—Chapter 4 addresses environmental conditions such as weather, water, terrain, and animal and plant life.
- Equipment—Chapter 5 discusses technical and nontechnical equipment, clothing, communication devices, and safety equipment.
- Transportation—Chapter 6 addresses the transporting of participants to and from activity sites.

As you review the scenarios in this book, you'll discover that the most serious incidents resulted from a combination of factors (which will be discussed later). This chapter presents a definition of risk management in the context of guided and adventure programs, followed by a brief discussion of the components of a risk management plan. Included in this discussion are a number of theories, or models, for assessing risk that can be used to analyze the scenarios in this text and answer the questions that follow them.

RISK MANAGEMENT MODELS

Risk management is a key responsibility of outdoor adventure programs and is the focus of this text. Risk management is a dynamic, ongoing process of evaluating the potential for risk and determining the best methods to address those risks (van der Smissen, 1990). It also helps adventure programs and guide services provide the programming they desire; fulfill the moral and ethical responsibility to keep their clients reasonably free from harm; and protect program assets, employees, and the program's professional image (van der Smissen, 1990). The goal of any risk management program should be to reduce the probability and severity of accidents and injuries, and to minimize liability exposure to the organization.

Part of a risk management plan is identifying the risks for the activity and location. What risks might you encounter while taking part in a ropes course?
Photo courtesy Aram Attarian.

For the purpose of this book, **risk management** is defined as the systematic application of management policies, standards, and **procedures** to identify, analyze, assess, treat, and monitor risk. Recording and analyzing accidents, incidents, and **misadventures** is an important part of this process. Every program should have a risk management plan. Components of the plan include ways to (1) identify risks (hazard assessment), (2) evaluate risks (the frequency and severity of incidents), and (3) control or adjust risks (retain, reduce, avoid, and transfer). These components are discussed next.

Risk Identification, or Hazard Assessment

Accident causation theories help programmers understand the factors and processes involved in accidents so they can develop accident prevention strategies. These theories are based on various perceptions of the accident process. Two of the causation theories adapted for use in guided and adventure programs are the domino theory (Heinrich, 1936) and the dynamics of accidents theory (Hale, 1983).

Domino Theory

The domino theory suggests that risk factors interact in multiple and unpredictable ways and can connect in a chain of events leading up to an accident. Heinrich (1936) used the analogy of toppling dominos to explain the cause of accidents. When the first domino falls, it strikes the next, and so on, resulting in a chain of events. However, if a single domino is removed, the entire process stops.

Heinrich identified five stages of accident causation. The first stage, *social environment and ancestry*, includes anything that may produce undesirable traits in people—for example, genetics, poor parenting or socializing, and an unhealthy subculture are all examples of characteristics that can negatively influence people and lead to stage 2. Stage 2, *faults of a person*, addresses the personal characteristics that are favorable to accidents. For instance, a poor attitude or ignorance could lead to a disregard for safety. *Unsafe act or condition* is the third stage of the model and is often the beginning of a specific incident. The fourth stage is the *accident*. An **accident** is an incident that happens unexpectedly and unintentionally, typically resulting in damage or injury. The final stage, *injury,* is the unfortunate outcome of some accidents.

Meyer (1978) adapted the domino theory and applied it to adventure programs (see figure 1.1). Meyer's stage 1 (background) includes the

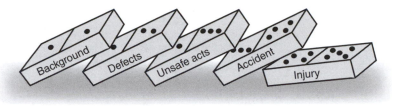

Figure 1.1 The domino theory.

Adapted from D. Meyer, 1978, *Accident control and reporting responsibilities*. Unpublished manuscript (Asheville, NC: North Carolina Outward Bound School).

program environment (e.g., weather, food, amount of rest, daily activities); stage 2 (defects of the person) comprises lack of skill, knowledge, coordination, or judgment, as well as poor attitude. Stage 3 (unsafe acts or conditions) includes specific unsafe behavior or conditions surrounding a particular activity; stage 4 (accident) is the combination of the previous factors, which generally triggers an accident; and stage 5 is injury, although not all accidents result in injury. Meyer emphasized the need to recognize unsafe acts and unsafe conditions, suggesting that accident control relies almost totally on removing unsafe acts or conditions.

Dynamics of Accidents Theory

Hale (1983) created the dynamics of accidents theory to explain how accidents happen by examining the interaction between two wide-ranging categories: subjective, or human-caused, factors, and **objective, or environmental, factors.** We can manage or control subjective factors (e.g., by recognizing **hazards** and making decisions and judgment calls), whereas we have limited or no control over objective, or environmental, factors (i.e., acts of God). Objective hazards include natural phenomena such as thunderstorms; swift, cold water; and gravity.

Subjective and objective factors exist independently of each other. At times, however, these factors interact and create what is commonly referred to as **accident potential**. This interaction is illustrated in figure 1.2 on page 6. The area in which the two categories overlap has the highest potential for accidents. Take, for example, a climber standing on a summit during a thunderstorm. The climber has made a poor decision (subjective factor) to be on the summit during a thunderstorm (objective factor). As a result, the climber has a high probability of being struck by lightning (accident potential). Both environmental and subjective factors are discussed further in chapters 3 and 4.

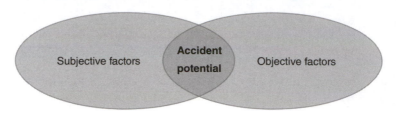

Figure 1.2 Dynamics of accidents theory.

Adapted from A. Hale, 1983, *Safety management for outdoor program leaders*. Unpublished manuscript.

Risk Evaluation

When managing the risks inherent in guided and adventure program activities, programmers must evaluate risk. **Risk evaluation** is a component of risk management in which decisions are made about the importance and acceptability of risk. A useful risk evaluation tool is the potential frequency and severity of loss model (Cuskelly & Auld, 1989). This model helps conceptualize the appropriate action(s) to take to mitigate risk depending on the (1) likelihood of an incident occurring and (2) the potential seriousness of an incident (see figure 1.3). *Frequency* refers to how often an incident may be expected to happen. *Severity* suggests the state or extent of injury resulting from a particular incident. For example, a commercial whitewater guide service conducted a review of rafting injuries for their organization and noted that six guests (almost one-third) were injured at a rapid named Ferry Hole over the course of a year (n=19, the total number of injured for the year). For the guide service, six (31%) is a high number or *frequency* of injured guests at this particular rapid. In addition, most of the injuries reported at this site were minor *(not severe)*, consisting of contusions and abrasions.

Given this information, the risk manager of the outfitter can use the potential frequency and severity of loss model to help her decide whether or not the company should continue to run Ferry Hole rapid.

She will note that frequency of injury at Ferry Hole rapid is high and the severity of reported injury is low. By noting high frequency and low severity in the upper left hand corner of the potential frequency and severity of loss model the outfitter should identify ways the guide service can *reduce* their exposure. In other words, what the outfitter can do to reduce the number of injuries at Ferry Hole. In this case, the outfitter discouraged her guides from surfing the standing wave beneath the drop which was identified as the cause for many of the injuries (guests were colliding with one another in the raft or being

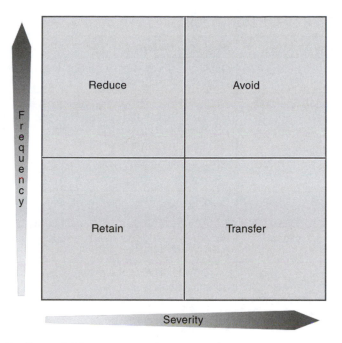

Figure 1.3   Potential frequency and severity of loss model.

Adapted from G. Cuskelly and C.J. Auld, 1989, "Retain, reduce, transfer or avoid? Risk management in sport organizations," *The ACHPER National Journal* 23: 17-20.

ejected into the water where they were exposed to rocks in the river). Guides now run the rapid and do not stop to surf the wave at the bottom of the drop. The next year's injury report revealed no reported injuries at Ferry Hole rapid.

If guests received more serious or *severe* injuries (dislocations and fractures) more frequently, the guide service may elect to *avoid* (high frequency/high severity, upper right-hand quadrant) Ferry Hole rapid altogether.

Risk Control or Adjustment

Risk control involves implementing methods to reduce the amount of risk inherent in an activity. This usually involves putting into practice policies, standards, and procedures, and making physical changes to activities or activity sites. Risk control strategies (see table 1.1 on page 8) should emphasize staffing, the conduct of activities and the management of services, participants, maintenance, the environment, warnings, standards, information and documentation, public relations, and equipment

Table 1.1 Risk Control Strategies

Risk control strategy	Focus of strategy
Staffing	Qualifications, staff/client ratios, training and preparation, supervision
Conduct of activities and management of services	Mission statement, goals, objectives, policies, client evaluation and preparation, group control, emergency action plans, transportation, risk awareness, standards of care
Participants	Characteristics and condition, supervision, emergency procedures
Maintenance	Buildings, grounds, equipment, inspections, human behavior management
Environment (built and natural)	Hazard evaluation, area ethics, appropriateness for participant skill level
Warnings	Hazards inherent in the activities presented, potential injuries
Standards	Compliance with industry standards
Information and documentation	Medical history, agreement to participate, permission to participate, permits, other documents required by program
Public relations	Plan of action to address problems that arise from accidents, incidents, and other issues
Equipment	Appropriateness for activity; technical, protective, and safety equipment; appropriate clothing for activity; record keeping

Adapted from van der Smissen 1990.

(van der Smissen, 1990). Adventure and guide service programmers have a number of options to proactively manage, reduce, or eliminate risk by retaining, reducing, avoiding, or transferring it. These approaches are described in the following sections.

Risk Retention

Risk retention can be passive (i.e., the organization is unaware of the risk) or active (i.e., the risk is identified and a decision is made to retain it and pay for any losses from the organization's own resources). When the frequency and severity of risk is low, program providers often retain the risk (the lower left-hand quadrant of the potential frequency and severity of loss model). Risk retention is a type of self-insurance whereby the organization assumes and accepts loss up to a certain point. An example of risk retention is a climbing guide who decides not to insure her personal climbing equipment. She bases her decision on the fact that the cost to replace her gear would be less than the insurance premiums she would pay over time.

Risk Reduction

When the severity of a potential risk remains low, but the overall frequency increases, organizations need to consider methods for reducing their exposure (upper left-hand quadrant of the potential frequency and severity of loss model). As an example, ankle sprains (low severity) are a common problem (high frequency) on many backpacking trips. Appropriate responses to reduce the number of ankle sprains might include providing specific boot requirements in preprogram equipment lists, making participants aware of the problems associated with poor footwear selection, or providing preprogram ankle strengthening exercises.

Risk Avoidance

Finally, when the frequency and severity of risk are both high, program providers and guide services should consider canceling the program or activity (upper right-hand quadrant of the potential frequency and severity of loss model). For example, an organization may decide to eliminate its mountain biking program because riders have sustained too many serious injuries such as fractures and dislocations.

Risk Transfer

As the severity of risk potential increases, organizations cannot afford to retain their risk and so must transfer it to others. Transferring risk is the best option when the frequency of risk potential is low, but the severity of a potential incident is high (lower right-hand quadrant of the potential frequency and severity of loss model). Traditionally, transfer usually occurs through the purchase of liability insurance. Requiring participants to show proof of medical insurance or having them purchase rescue and evacuation insurance will relieve the program or guide service from having to pay medical, rescue, and evacuation costs for an injured student or client.

Subcontracting services is another method of transferring risk; for instance, leasing vehicles may transfer loss away from the user and to the owner. Educating participants about the risk inherent in an activity and adopting a process by which they agree to accept that risk (e.g., sign an assumption of risk form) is another approach to risk transfer.

INCIDENT COUNTERMEASURES

An **incident countermeasure** is an action or actions taken in response to an injury or event or prevent it from recurring. For example, after a near drowning during a stream crossing, a program administrator decides to teach stream crossing techniques in staff or in-service trainings, require staff to choose another area at which to cross, or eliminate the stream crossing to prevent the incident from recurring.

The Haddon matrix, developed to manage injuries associated with motor vehicle accidents, is a good incident countermeasure model for guided and adventure programs (Haddon, 1972). Haddon was a well-known figure in the U.S. National Highway Traffic Safety Administration and Insurance Institute for Highway Safety. The original matrix consisted of four columns: (1) host (or the person affected by the injury); (2) agent/vehicle (the energy transferred to the host by either an instrument, such as a firearm, or a motor vehicle); (3) physical environment (elements of the physical setting that contribute to injury-producing incidents); and (4) social environment (e.g., community norms, policies). Rows in the matrix are labeled *preevent, event,* and *postevent.* This model is an important tool for risk managers because it conceptualizes the causes of injury and identifies potential preventive strategies.

Table 1.2 shows the application of a modified version of the Haddon matrix to the risks associated with rock climbing. The value of the matrix is that each cell illustrates an area in which interventions can be undertaken to improve climber safety. For example, the top-left cell, representing the climber in the preactivity phase, lists awareness of the climber's medical and health history, modifications to training, and a hazard briefing as ways to reduce incident rates.

Incident Reporting as Injury Countermeasure

Many guided and adventure programs have instituted incident reporting systems to record details of incidents, accidents, or near misses that occur during a program to participants or staff members. An **incident** is a minor event or condition, whereas an accident is an incident that happens unexpectedly and unintentionally, typically resulting in damage or injury. A **near miss** is an unplanned event that did not result in injury, illness, or damage but had the potential to do so. The purpose of the incident report is to document the details of the occurrence while they are fresh in the minds of those who witnessed the event.

Table 1.2 Modified Haddon Matrix Applied to Risks Associated With Rock Climbing

Activity phase	Host (climbers)	Agent/vehicle (equipment)	Physical environment (climbing site)	Social environment (program culture, policies, procedures)
Preactivity phase	• Obtain medical or health history. • Provide appropriate training (knots, belaying technique, equipment use). • Give a hazard briefing. • Obtain weather report.	Inspect all climbing equipment (repair or replace as needed).	• Conduct site assessment (anchors, hazards, access/egress). • Establish evacuation routes. • Determine appropriateness given students' skill sets. • Obtain weather report.	• Ensure that staff are familiar with local operating procedures. • Implement policies appropriately.
Activity phase	• Provide general supervision. • Offer progressive instruction. • Evaluate student energy levels, pace of activity.	• Ensure that safety equipment is being used properly. • Evaluate anchors.	Establish helmet zones and safety or community zones.	• Ensure that climber and belayer systems are checked by staff prior to climbing. • Ensure that assessment techniques are appropriate.
Postactivity phase	• Additional training needed. • Student needs met.	• Obtain additional equipment as needed. • Catalog and store equipment appropriately.	• Reassess site for appropriateness.	• Reevaluate emergency action plan. • Reevaluate necessary medical and rescue skills.

Incident reporting is an important risk management tool that identifies preventable incidents and measures the effect of actions taken to reduce incidents. This information may also be useful when dealing with liability issues stemming from the incident. An important requirement for the effective reporting of all incidents, and especially near misses, is an open culture in which outdoor leaders and guides are willing to report. Senior staff members need to model this process. Incident reports usually involve four steps: collecting data, identifying trends, creating change, and monitoring and evaluating. (See table 1.3 for the details of each step.)

Safety Committee as Injury Countermeasure

Many adventure programs and guide services have formed safety committees to improve the health and safety of both staff and participants and provide oversight for any decisions involving risk management. In some cases a safety committee is a requirement for program accreditation (Association for Experiential Education, 2009). The safety committee is usually composed of administrators, field staff, and professionals from the organization's larger community who work with the program as advisors (e.g., local physicians, attorneys). Safety committees are an added value to the organization because they get employees interested, involved, and focused on reducing accidents and provide a safe venue where people can express their concerns, ask safety-related questions, or offer suggestions for improving both the safety and quality of programs.

Safety and Quality Reviews as Injury Countermeasures

In addition to establishing safety committees, guided or adventure program providers should conduct safety and quality reviews. The safety and quality review is a "process for assessing the safety status of an organization that involves a team of qualified people making a brief visit to gather data. The reviewers provide feedback designed to upgrade the program and may make specific recommendations on safety matters" (Wade & Fischesser, 1988, p. 2). Reviews should be conducted on an annual or biannual basis or as determined by the program administrator, safety committee, board of directors, or governing body (if the program is a national organization). A comprehensive safety and quality review should examine various program components including participant screening, staff or guide qualifications, management systems, program activities, **emergency** procedures, logistics, facilities, and transportation (Wade & Fischesser, 1988).

The review ends when the review team, program administrators, and safety committee members discuss the results of the review. A final report that contains a list of recommendations and suggestions for program improvement, and both positive and negative observations, is written

Table 1.3 Steps for Incident Reporting

Step	Criteria for incident reporting
Step 1: Collecting data	• Requires more than simple first aid (i.e., more than a bandage or blister dressing). • Requires more than cursory staff attention. • Requires follow-up by staff in the field. • Requires follow up by a medical professional. • Requires follow-up by a therapist, psychologist, or social worker. • Requires use of prescription medications. • Interferes with the subject's active participation. • Requires evacuation from the field. • Results in the loss of at least one calendar day of participation in program activities following the day the injury or illness occurs. • Results in a near miss. • Significantly affects the participant's or group's experience (behaviorally or motivationally). • Has the potential to involve an insurance claim, a lawsuit, or public relations. • Involves a vehicle. • Requires early departures for behavioral, motivational, psychological, or medical reasons. • Requires evacuation from the field via non-program resources (e.g., helicopter, fixed wing, horse, private vehicle). • Requires the use of a field communication device. • Involves a violation of policy; local operating procedure; or local, state, or federal law.
Step 2: Identifying trends	• Activities with significant incident rates • Number of staff members involved • Number of students involved • Types and frequency of injuries • Activities in which incidents are most likely • Activity location • Role of preexisting conditions • Drop-out for medical, behavioral, or motivational reasons
Step 3: Creating change	• Determine which incidents are preventable. • Modify the activity. • Change or modify equipment. • Change policy. • Offer better staff training. • Take more comprehensive participant medical histories. • Change the evaluation procedure.
Step 4: Monitoring and evaluating	Following change, retest the approach, policy, etc., to note any difference. If no change is noted, then explore other factors.

Adapted from Haddad 2010.

by the review team leader, approved by the review team members, and presented to the program administrators.

EMERGENCY ACTION PLANS

A program's **emergency action plan** is a set of procedures designed to direct an organization's response to an accident. Program managers and others who will be involved in the response need to review and approve these procedures. Every accident has its own unique set of characteristics. By being aware of this, program providers can develop strategies for responding to accidents. Everyone involved in the organization—administrators, guides, instructors, and participants—should know that an emergency action plan exists and understand how to initiate it. When designed and implemented properly, an emergency action plan (1) assigns responsibilities for action to be taken both *during* and *after* an emergency; (2) provides **guidelines** based on the nature of the emergency, and (3) identifies resources for emergency response.

SUMMARY

Risk management is a dynamic process for reducing incidents to an acceptable level and minimizing the consequences to the organization, staff, and participants in the event an accident occurs. Accident causation theories help us to understand the factors and processes involved in accidents and develop strategies for preventing them. Effective risk management focuses on identifying, evaluating, and controlling risk. The domino theory (Heinrich, 1936) uses the analogy of toppling dominos to explain the cause of accidents. It describes five stages of accident causation: the social environment and ancestry, the faults of a person, an unsafe act or condition, the accident, and injury. Meyer (1978) adapted the domino theory and applied it to adventure programs by emphasizing the need to recognize unsafe acts and unsafe conditions, suggesting that accidents can be controlled or minimized by removing unsafe acts or conditions.

Hale's dynamics of accidents theory (1983) explains how accidents happen by examining the interactions between subjective (human-caused) and objective (environmental) factors. Safety for most programs can be maximized by applying proper program structure and management (Sagan, 1993).

Risk control strategies should focus on the hiring, firing, training, and evaluation of staff; how program activities are conducted; how the program manages the various services it offers; how it manages participants, information, and documentation; and how well it maintains equipment, adheres to standards, addresses environmental impacts and ethics, and conducts public relations.

Another risk control strategy is the potential frequency and severity of loss model (Cuskelly & Auld, 1989). This model defines the suitable action to take to alleviate risk depending on the likelihood of an incident occurring and the potential seriousness of an incident. The Hadden matrix (Haddon, 1964) is also an important tool for risk managers because it helps to conceptualize the causes of injury and identifies preventive strategies.

An incident reporting system identifies preventable incidents and measures the effect of actions taken to reduce them. An open culture in which outdoor leaders and guides are willing to report is an important requirement for effective incident reporting. The formation of a safety committee adds value to an organization because committee members can get involved and focus on reducing accidents, express their concerns, ask safety-related questions, and offer suggestions for improving both the safety and quality of the program. Programs should also make an effort to conduct annual safety and quality reviews. A well-developed program safety and quality review examines various program elements including participant screening, staff qualifications, management systems, program activities, emergency procedures, logistics, facilities, and transportation.

All programs should have an emergency action plan to direct the organization's response to an accident. These plans need to be reviewed and approved by program managers and others who will be involved in the response.

Chapter 2

Risk Management Legal Terms and Concepts

Educating instructional staff and guides on basic legal terms and concepts is an important risk management measure. Staff members who are familiar with legal terms and concepts often conduct themselves in a more professional manner, exhibit a positive attitude toward risk management, make more conscious decisions, engage in dialogue with others, and are prepared to comply with policies and laws, thereby preventing injuries and litigation.

A comprehensive overview of recreation law is beyond the scope of this book. Instead, this chapter discusses a number of legal terms and concepts that are commonly used or referenced in the context of risk management in the field of guided and adventure programs and sports. Additional definitions, concepts, and legal questions can be explored and answered by reviewing the legal literature or consulting an attorney.

CONTRACTS

A logical place to get started is contracts. When deciding to participate in a guided or adventure program activity, participants enter into a contract. A **contract** is an agreement between two or more parties in which an offer is made and accepted, and each party benefits. The agreement can be formal, informal, written, oral, or understood. Basically, the law provides adequate solutions to participants who are injured when instructors and guides fail to carry out their promises or legal obligations, whether they are stated or promised or not. In most cases the participant who has been injured brings suit against the person who failed to perform (van der Smissen, 1990). Waivers and releases are common contracts in the outdoor and adventure program industry; they are intended to absolve the program in advance for a wrong that may occur later.

TORT LAW

Tort law provides the legal foundation for activities conducted by an adventure program or guide service. The word *tort* originated from the Latin word *tortus,* which means "twisted" or "distorted." *Black's Law Dictionary* (Garner, 2009) defines tort as "a civil wrong for which a remedy may be obtained, usually in the form of damages; a breach of duty that the law imposes on everyone in the same relation to one another as those involved in a given transaction" (p. 1496).

A successful tort suit results in a judgment of liability. Such a judgment normally requires the defendant to compensate the plaintiff financially.

Torts can be either intentional or unintentional. Lawsuits that involve adventure or guiding organizations focus primarily on unintentional torts such as manufacturer's liability, nuisance, and negligence.

Negligence

Negligence is commonly defined as the failure to use ordinary care: failing to do what a person of ordinary prudence would have done under the same or similar circumstances. Negligence is a legal principle in common and criminal law and refers to some kind of a civil wrongdoing; it is an important concept of law that should be understood by outdoor leaders and guides.

The existence of negligence depends on the circumstances connected to each case. To prove negligence, the participant or plaintiff must show that (1) the guide or instructor (the defendant) owed the plaintiff a duty of care (or was legally responsible to the plaintiff); (2) the defendant breached that duty or failed to perform a required task; (3) the breach of duty was the cause of the defendant's injury (referred to as proximate cause); and (4) the breach resulted in mental, physical, or financial damage to the plaintiff (Garner, 2009). In some cases the court may consider whether the plaintiff's own negligence played a role in the damage or injury. This is referred to as contributory negligence and may prevent the plaintiff from receiving compensation. In some cases the plaintiff's own negligence (comparative negligence) may reduce the damages recoverable from a defendant.

Duty of Care

Duty of care is an obligation to act toward others and the public with the degree of watchfulness, attention, caution, and prudence that a reasonable person in similar circumstances would have. If a person's actions do not meet this standard of care, then the acts are considered negligent and any resultant damages may be claimed in a lawsuit for negligence.

Standard of Care

Standard of care is a term that is commonly used in risk management. Whereas duty of care refers to an obligation to act toward others and the public, **standard of care** refers to the degree of attentiveness, caution, and prudence that a reasonable person in the same circumstances would exercise. Failure to meet the standard is negligence, and the person proven negligent is liable for any damages caused by such negligence.

What standard of care would an organization have for this rock climber?

The standard is not subject to a precise definition and is judged on a case-by-case basis.

Certain **standards** for guides and outdoor leaders are established by professionals in the outdoor industry. Other nonprofessional standards may be established through laws and regulations. Also, the standard of care may vary based on the relationship between the parties. For example, a higher standard of care is applied in situations involving a compensated service (i.e., fee involved) than a gratuitous favor (no charge).

To meet the standard of care, guide and adventure program administrators and staff should make an effort to develop and deliver a safe and relevant educational curriculum; become familiar with and implement **industry standards** and guidelines; hire qualified and competent staff; create and implement a risk management plan; educate and make participants aware of and have them acknowledge the risks inherent in the program; and maintain appropriate staff and participant records (Cloutier & Valade, n.d.).

Guides and program staff are responsible for their participants. Participants look to them for instruction, guidance, and support so they can participate safely in program activities. Typically, this requires that the guide or instructor anticipate dangers, mistakes, and pitfalls and attempt to ensure that these risks do not materialize. The greater the degree of risk, the greater the instructor's obligation to anticipate and avoid harm.

Causation

The third element that proves negligence is the determination that a breach of duty was the cause (causation) of the defendant's injury. **Causation** is defined as "the causing or producing of an effect" (Garner, 2009, p. 212). Remember, to prove negligence, the plaintiff must show that a relationship existed (**proximate cause**) between what the defendant did or didn't do and the plaintiff's accident or damage. The **foreseeability** feature of proximate cause is established by proving that the instructor or guide should have foreseen, or known in advance, that harm or injury may result from the negligent act regardless of what the participant guessed would happen. The ability of an instructor or guide to foresee a danger depends on a number of factors, including training and experience (Legal Dictionary, 2011). Consider the example of a mountain guide, who, to save time, decides to cross avalanche terrain with a group of participants knowing that the morning avalanche report stated a high avalanche danger. While the group is crossing the slope, it releases, injuring three participants and burying one resulting in death. This is an example of foreseeability. The guide, given her training, experience, and warning of avalanche, should have foreseen the danger and changed the route. This action may be deemed by the courts as negligence.

DUE DILIGENCE

Due diligence refers to precautions that a person or organization should take in light of the circumstances. For example, a guide organization should thoroughly check the medical history forms of all clients prior to the start of a program to ensure that they are adequately prepared for the program and that no medical concerns may prevent or curtail participation. If guides or instructors don't review medical history forms, and negative results come of their negligence, they can be held criminally liable.

DUTY TO WARN

Another important legal concept, **duty to warn**, states that one can be held liable for injuries caused to another when an opportunity existed to warn the other of a hazard and the person failed to do so. The nature and scope of the risks inherent in an adventure activity must be fully disclosed to all participants and staff prior to the start of the program. Unless the danger is obvious, the law imposes a duty to warn of reasonably foreseeable risks of harm. Participants who are not made aware of the

To fulfill its duty to warn, what dangers, obvious or hidden, of whitewater canoeing should an organization make potential participants aware of?
Photo courtesy of Keith Crawford.

risks cannot later be held to have assumed those risks. When disclosing risks, the guide or outdoor leader must consider the participant's age, skill level, and knowledge.

Duty to warn can be addressed by including an **assumption of risk** statement in the participant or client waiver and conducting a preactivity safety talk or briefing (see page 28 for more information on safety briefings) that identifies the risks inherent in the activity. In tort law, assumption of risk means that plaintiffs voluntarily accepted or exposed themselves to a risk of damage, injury, or loss, after learning that the condition or situation was clearly dangerous and nonetheless making the decision to act. In such cases, the defendant may raise the plaintiff's knowledge and appreciation of the danger as an affirmative defense. Successful use of assumption of risk as a positive defense results in a reduction or elimination of damages assessed against the defendant. This defense has been strictly limited in many states and is unavailable for certain types of actions, such as product liability cases.

SUMMARY

Understanding legal concepts and terminology is an important part of managing risk in guided and adventure programs. Guides and instructors with fundamental legal knowledge are better able to demonstrate a positive attitude toward managing risk, engage in dialogue with other professionals, and conform to policies and laws.

Chapter 3 introduces the various human resources (i.e., staff and participants) factors that play a role in risk management. It also introduces a variety of scenarios to explore the issues introduced by staff and participants that cause accidents.

Program Staff and Participants

Chapter 1 introduced the concept of subjective, or human-caused, factors that result in accidents. These factors usually originate from a guide, instructor, or participant who has made poor decisions, lacks good judgment, is deficient in the appropriate skills or knowledge, or is physically unfit. Unlike with objective factors, guides, leaders, and participants can manage or control subjective factors by becoming more experienced, skilled, and knowledgeable in areas in which they are deficient.

INSTRUCTORS AND GUIDES

Field instructors and guides are the people most directly able to ensure safety because of their training, experience, expertise, and continuous interaction with participants. In most adventure program settings, two or more staff members are assigned to **participants or groups,** and one is designated the lead instructor or head guide. The primary role of instructional staff or guides is to observe and anticipate hazards that the group may encounter, help participants deal with hazards, provide participants with appropriate training, and evaluate each program component, including co-instructor or guide performance.

The hiring, training, supervision, evaluation, and termination of instructors or guides are important risk management considerations for any adventure program or guide service. Instructors or guides should be hired based on their skills, knowledge, and experience and should meet the risk management, operational, and curriculum goals for each program activity (Association for Experiential Education, 2009).

STAFF TRAINING

Almost all adventure programs and guide services conduct some form of staff training. It usually includes both a returning staff session and a new staff session to introduce new hires to the program's philosophy, policies, and operations.

Staff training sessions should concentrate on enhancing the technical, educational, and people skills staff need to meet the program's standards. Training should provide feedback to staff and should continue throughout their tenure with the program. Training sessions help staff to judge whether they need more training for a specific skill or a better understanding of standard and local operating procedures, policies, course or program area information, paperwork requirements, and so on. New staff may receive verbal or written feedback on their performance by staff that have been with the company longer (mentors) or by administrators. Seasonal and periodic staff trainings (especially in specialized areas such as climbing, paddling, and challenge courses), workshops, and staff expeditions to enhance instructional or guiding skills are some of the ways programs upgrade the skills of their field staff (Niccolazzo, 2010).

Staff trainings should pay particular attention to enhancing skills, developing standards and procedures for activity areas, and to meeting land management agency requirements and mandates (e.g., permits, group size mandates, leader qualifications). In general, instructors and guides should be skilled professionals who are effective teachers and good facilitators with good judgment and decision-making skills. They also must be able to manage and assess risks, respond to emergencies, and exhibit strong professional and environmental ethics.

Staff Manuals

Every program should create a staff manual to provide field staff and guides with standard and local operating procedures, course or program area information, paperwork requirements (e.g., accident or incident forms, instructor or guide evaluations), pay scales, and hiring and promotion standards. Policies, safety guidelines, emergency protocols, and other risk management practices should also be included.

First Aid or Rescue Simulations

First aid or rescue simulations are valuable learning experiences that should be part of staff training. Simulations allow instructors or guides to practice first aid and search and rescue skills, become familiar (or re-familiarize themselves) with the program's emergency action plan, develop leadership and team-building skills, and improve their communication skills in a secure, supportive environment. They also offer the opportunity to experience the consequences of mistakes in a controlled setting. Effectively designed and implemented simulations improve knowledge, critical thinking, satisfaction, and confidence (Cooper et al., 2011).

Instructor or Guide Meetings

Instructor or guides meetings should be conducted prior to the start of the course or program, on a daily basis during the program, and at the culmination of the program. Pretrip meetings should focus on establishing goals and objectives and reviewing participant medical histories, expedition and evacuation routes, medical and emergency resources, campsite locations and water sources, weather forecasts, equipment needs, food and menus, snow conditions, water levels, transportation concerns, and other relevant topics as dictated by the type and location of the program or guide service. Once the program is underway, guides and instructors should make an effort to meet at the beginning or end of each day, prior to the start of activity, or during downtime to review the day, initiate contingency plans in the case of poor weather or terrain, evaluate participant needs, and so on. Postprogram meetings should focus on program evaluation, other end-of-program activities, and paperwork as dictated by the organization.

Safety Briefings

Before beginning any activity, the guide or instructor should give a safety briefing to all participants. The purpose of this briefing is to prepare everyone for emergencies that can occur during the activity. Commonly referred to as a safety talk, the briefing plays an important role in risk management. Safety talks provide program participants with relevant information to ensure a successful trip and keep guides and instructors up-to-date on safety procedures, equipment, and responsibilities. The guide or instructor giving a safety talk should refrain from using lingo or acronyms that new participants might not understand. This is crucial to ensure that participants understand the guidelines being discussed. When creating a safety talk, guides and instructors should consider the steps outlined in the following river safety talk:

1. **Introduce the topic.** *The purpose of this safety talk is to inform you about the actions you need to take if something goes wrong on the river today to rescue yourself or assist in the rescue of someone else.*

2. **Explain the dangers.** Describe the risks inherent in the activity (e.g., strainers, hydraulics, hypothermia, foot entrapment, whitewater swimmer's position, lightning).

3. **Explain the organization's policies** (e.g., personal flotation devices, also called swim vests, will be worn at all times by staff and participants when on the water).

4. **Tell stories.** Stories and personal experiences related to the topic being discussed are great for emphasizing points and keeping participants' attention.

5. **Ask questions** to make sure everyone understands.

Using the steps outlined in the river example, how would you plan a safety briefing for mountain biking?

Eyewire/Getty Images

6. **Document attendance.** At the end of the safety talk, ask participants to print their names and then sign an attendance sheet as a record that they attended the safety talk. File for your records.

PROGRAM PARTICIPANTS

Participant, or client, management is an important risk management component of any adventure program or guide service. Participant management involves meeting a participant's basic safety and psychological needs through adequate training and instruction. It requires good planning and management skills and begins well before participants arrive for the start of the program and continues until the program ends. Prior to arriving, participants should receive medical history and physical exam forms as well as personal clothing and equipment lists. They should be informed of the program's goals and requirements for physical conditioning and behavior, and the consequences of not meeting these requirements. Emergency contact and insurance information, travel information, and an explanation of the organization's refund policy should also be sent to participants prior to the start of the program.

Program participants can enhance everyone's safety by being honest about how comfortable they are undertaking certain tasks or activities;

by following instructions and using good judgment; by letting staff or others know when they feel endangered or see others in danger; and by reporting any safety issues they observe to staff and managers.

The following is a checklist of risk management tasks to perform before the program begins:

- Review participant medical histories.
- Review participant health and fitness statements.
- Review participants' medical insurance information.
- Send participants clothing and equipment lists.
- Review emergency contact information.
- Establish the participant/staff ratio.
- Ensure that activities are age appropriate.
- Ensure that equipment is age appropriate.
- Plan menus and buy food.

The following is a checklist of risk management tasks to perform during the program:

- Monitor the skill development of participants.
- Create an environment of emotional and physical safety by managing behavior.
- Conduct safety briefings before the start of every activity throughout the program.
- Establish and follow a daily routine.
- Evaluate participant energy levels.
- Provide participants with the emergency action plan.
- Ensure that equipment is sized to fit individual participants.
- Build rapport.
- Observe, assess, and understand participants.
- Teach interpersonal and conflict resolution skills.
- Create an inclusive culture that embraces diversity.

The following is a checklist of risk management tasks to perform at the conclusion of the program:

- Conduct exit interviews.
- Conduct a program evaluation.

- Follow up with any incidents.
- Write a program report.
- Maintain, repair, or replace equipment.
- Conduct a staff evaluation.

SUMMARY

Instructors and guides play an important role in controlling the subjective risks that participants are exposed to by attempting to balance the level of risk with the level of participant ability and experience. They do this by presenting the curriculum in a manner that leads from simple to more complex tasks and by consciously striving to manage the level of risk to which participants, instructors, and other staff are exposed. Instructors and guides should also, to the best of their ability and training, address the specific needs of the population they serve (e.g., medical, physical, emotional, psychological).

Program participants can also influence safety. Prior to being accepted into a program, participants should be screened to determine that their skill levels are appropriate for the program and that they have no medical or psychological problems that may endanger themselves or others.

Responding to Emergencies

One afternoon a pair of climbing guides from Pisgah Outdoor Adventures, North Carolina, and their clients (ten 15- to 17-year-old males) hiked to the summit of the Devil's Courthouse.* Because of the topography, all of the climbs were accessed from the summit and top managed. To do this, guides set up top ropes and then lowered their clients to the base of the climb where they proceeded to climb back to the summit.

Andre, one of the guides, had limited knowledge of the climbing area and decided to down-climb (unroped) to a large ledge approximately halfway down the northeast face. His goal was to explore the face below because he was convinced that there were some new climbs that could be bottom managed. After a few minutes of walking around the ledge, and satisfied with his reconnaissance, he began to ascend. After climbing several feet on almost vertical rock, his foot slipped and he fell the approximately 80 feet (24 m) to the ground sustaining life-threatening injuries. The group heard him yell as he fell and then crash through the tree canopy below. Dave, the other guide, realizing what had happened, took a few deep breaths and a moment to gather his thoughts and initiate a response.

Put yourself in Dave's shoes and initiate your program's emergency action plan to respond to this almost tragic accident.

*Rock climbing is no longer permitted at the Devil's Courthouse due to resource impacts.

QUESTIONS

1. What policies does your program have to avoid situations like this?

2. How would you respond to this situation? Using your program's emergency action plan as a template, begin your response to this accident.

3. Using Google Maps, locate the Devil's Courthouse area and identify the nearest evacuation routes, county sheriff, emergency services, and hospitals.

4. What role, if any, should the participants play in this scenario?

Open-Toed Shoes

Kate was working as a climbing instructor at a camp for girls. One of her responsibilities was to lead multipitch routes on Real Big Mountain. After spending most of June climbing in her approach shoes, Kate decided to make the climbing more challenging by climbing in her open-toed hiking sandals.

One morning, during the approach to a climb, Kate stubbed the great toe of her left foot on an exposed tree root. She experienced some pain and continued the climb. She climbed most of the day in her open-toed hiking sandals. The following morning, while walking to the dining hall, Kate experienced a sharp, persistent pain in the injured toe. The pain continued throughout the day. She finally visited the camp nurse, who noted that the toe might be broken. Kate drove herself to a nearby medical clinic and had her toe X-rayed. The X-ray revealed a fractured great toe. The toe was immobilized, and Kate was unable to climb for the rest of the summer.

QUESTIONS

1. When is the use of open-toed shoes appropriate?

2. Should programs have a policy about the use of open-toed shoes? Why or why not?

3. Should staff and participants have different requirements concerning policies and gear? Explain your answer.

4. Create an open-toed shoe policy for your program.

5. What are additional implications beyond the fact that Kate was unable to work for the remainder of the summer?

Returning Staff

Decreased employee retention rates in outdoor adventure programs have led some program administrators to risk the hiring of unfit, unqualified, or former staff to fill the gaps left by nonreturning or burned-out field instructors. The Outdoor Experience School (OES) is no exception. Like many other outdoor adventure programs, OES administrators have been having difficulty hiring and retaining qualified field instructors. Recently, the staffing coordinator has been asking former staff who live within a 100-mile radius of OES if they would be interested in working on an occasional basis—mostly, to lead four- and eight-day courses. Courses are the natural area or areas where the program is conducted.

Two former staff members were recently contacted and agreed to work a single eight-day course. One of them had not worked for OES for three years and had limited experience in the course area. She was paired with a second-year staff member who also had limited experience in the course area. The other former staff member had not worked for six years and was paired with a highly experienced instructor.

Both of the former instructors were sent copies of the OES standard and local operating procedures and policy manual. Course components included a multiday expedition, rock climbing, and a high ropes course. Each instructor pair had two full days to plan their courses before students arrived.

Both courses ran smoothly. However, a number of incidents were reported, with over half involving staff members. Further review revealed that each incident involving staff could be attributed to their lengthy absence. Both instructors admitted that after being gone three to six years, they were no longer familiar with the procedures as many had been instituted since they last worked.

QUESTIONS

1. Why is this scenario a risk management issue? Explain your answer.
2. How can program directors work with administrators to reduce employee turnover?
3. What kind of incentives can be offered to employees to retain them?
4. How can the above staffing approach (hiring former staff members that have been absent from the program for a length of time) be made more effective?
5. Conduct an informal online survey by contacting guide and outdoor adventure programs to determine the significance of the staffing issues plaguing some outdoor adventure programs.

Methicillin-Resistant Staphylococcus Aureus

Methicillin-resistant staphylococcus aureus (MRSA) is a bacterium responsible for difficult-to-treat infections in humans. It first appears on the skin as a reddish rash with lesion(s) that looks like pimples or small boils.

According to reports, Lynn Jacobs (15) was not sick before the start of her Adventure Alternative program on April 1. About midway through the program, on April 6, she noted a small boil on her leg and reported it to one of her instructors. Within a day, she wrote in her journal that she was "having headaches, chills and vomiting" and was "having trouble hiking."

Eventually, the pain spread to her knee and hip. Her instructors, both trained as wilderness first responders, monitored her condition. They gave her ibuprofen and encouraged her to continue in the program. Lynn's condition turned serious the following day, when she could no longer control her bodily functions. Lynn continued to receive ibuprofen and an over-the-counter antidiarrhea medicine.

On April 10, one of the instructors noted that Lynn hadn't eaten for 24 hours. She helped her drink some water and decided to call base camp to report Lynn's condition. Base camp advised the group to stay put and immediately initiated an evacuation. But it was too late. Lynn was pronounced dead at the scene of what was later determined to be a methicillin-resistant staph infection.

QUESTIONS

1. Conduct a short Internet search on MRSA. Describe it in detail and list ways program providers can be proactive in managing this public health issue.

2. What potential impact does this bacterium have on outdoor adventure programs? Explain your answer.

3. Write a policy for evacuating a student or instructor from the field in the event of a life-threatening injury or illness.

4. How will you address this issue in staff training?

5. Are there other similar illnesses that program providers should be concerned with?

Accidents, Incidents, and Misadventures

Peanut Allergy

Peanut butter, gorp, and other foods containing peanuts are common menu items on most backcountry food lists. Unfortunately, peanut allergies are on the rise, especially in children. It has been estimated that, in the United States, the number of children with peanut allergy doubled between 1997 and 2002. Peanut allergy is not only a common food allergy, but also one of the most dangerous, causing severe anaphylactic reactions (Peanut Allergy, 2010). Some people are so sensitive that they have reactions to eating only trace amounts of peanuts, as the following scenario portrays.

A group of students (14- and 15-year-olds) from the Outdoor Experience School (OES) were anticipating the finish of the backpacking section of their course, so they left camp early without breakfast. Around 10:00 a.m., some of the students became hungry so they stopped for a snack. One student (with a peanut allergy) saw the other students passing a snack mix around. She had eaten all of her specially prepared peanut-free mix, so she pulled some pieces of dried fruit out of the communal mix, which contained peanuts. The fruit she ate contained enough peanut trace to set off an anaphylactic reaction.

At 10:14 a.m., the student stopped, dropped her pack, and complained that her throat "felt funny." This was followed by a rapid onset of signs and symptoms of a systemic allergic reaction. The instructors tried to calm her breathing and decided to call the OES base camp. Base camp was able to arrange an evacuation at the nearest road. The instructors administered the first dose of epinephrine at 10:18 a.m. with Benadryl immediately following. The signs and symptoms did not change. By this time, the girl's right eye was nearly swollen shut, her breathing was labored, and she was incapable of speech. A second dose of epinephrine was administered at 10:23 a.m. The labored breathing continued, and she was visibly shaking and had clenched hands. She could say only the first syllable of her name at 10:29 a.m.

By 10:38 a.m. the student was able to breathe deeply. The swelling in her eye had decreased, although she was still shaking. Base camp was contacted again at 10:40 a.m., and the instructors began to walk the student out. At 10:50 a.m., after the student had walked approximately 100 meters, the signs and symptoms returned, so the instructors administered a third dose of epinephrine. At 11:06 a.m., two EMS crew members arrived; they administered epinephrine via IV and gave the student albuterol. A helicopter arrived at 11:50 a.m., and the student arrived at the hospital at 12:14 p.m.

QUESTIONS

1. Did the instructors do everything they could to prevent this situation from occurring? Explain your answer.

2. What are some steps to take to prevent a situation like this from happening?

3. Does your program have a protocol in place for injecting epinephrine? Administering albuterol?

4. If your program has a protocol in place, please discuss it with your group.

5. If your program does not have a protocol, develop one. What are some of the barriers to creating medical protocols?

6. What are additional allergies field instructors and guides should be aware of? How are these dealt with in backcountry settings?

Lost Student

During a high school backpacking trip in the American Southwest, Carlos (16) stepped off the trail to urinate and in the process the rest of his group continued by him. The group continued down the trail approximately a quarter of a mile (0.4 km) and took the right fork in the trail that led down to a stream. Here the group stopped for a well-deserved rest and lunch.

About 15 minutes had passed when one of the group members realized that Carlos had not rejoined the group. The instructors conducted a hasty search on the trail ahead thinking that Carlos had missed the fork in the trail. They were unsuccessful. After 30 minutes the entire group was involved in the search. A plan was initiated that involved regrouping at the stream after 90 minutes. During the search, one of the search groups ran into a lone hiker who said that he spoke to Carlos at a trail shelter where he and his partner had stayed the previous night. The shelter was a 30-minute walk from where the group had stopped for lunch.

Carlos told the hiker that he was with a larger group and that he had become separated from them when he stopped to relieve himself. The hiker had his partner stay with Carlos, while he ran off to look for the group. One of the instructors accompanied the hiker back to the shelter to retrieve Carlos and reunite him with the group.

QUESTIONS

1. What are some practices or procedures that should have been in place to prevent this incident?
2. How should a hasty search be conducted?
3. Develop a pre-hike briefing on what to do if you get lost.

Poor Route Finding

Eight teenagers and two instructors from the Rocky Mountain Summits (RMS) program left July 14 for a 10-day backpacking and climbing trip. One week into the program, the hikers approached their destination, Tall Peak, and set up camp nearby. Doug (head instructor) and Janie (assistant instructor) had never been to the area before. The following morning, Doug decided to leave camp early to recon a major crossing of the river that the group would encounter later in the day. The river was running above normal as a result of heavy snowmelt, and this had Doug concerned. He and Janie decided that they would meet at the Pinnacle, a local landmark a few miles north of their current location, do the river crossing, set up their base camp, and spend a couple of days rock climbing on Manzanita Peak.

Doug left with some food, water, and the group's only cell phone in his pack. He made good time on his hike to the river and was able to find a good place to cross. Later that afternoon, Doug arrived at the Pinnacle to meet Janie and the students. As dusk approached, Doug became worried because the group hadn't shown up. He decided that if the group didn't show up by the next morning, he would search for them. When they still hadn't arrived in the morning, he searched for most of the day.

It is easy to become disoriented in unfamiliar wooded or hilly areas. What would you do to prepare yourself and others to hike in an unfamiliar area?

Frustrated and scared, Doug finally contacted his program director (PD) at RMS. The PD told Doug to stay put and that he would send additional RMS staff to help him search.

Later that morning, RMS staff arrived and continued searching for the missing group with no luck. Later the next day, RMS decided to contact the sheriff's department. The local TV station also arrived on the scene. At this point, the RMS director decided that it would be in their best interest to contact the students' parents to apprise them of the situation.

The sheriff's department and local search and rescue teams began searching a 75-square-mile (194 sq km) area with no luck. The RMS group had been missing for three full days when the sheriff's department received a call that the group had been found walking along a state highway. Evidently, the group had become confused on their way to the Pinnacle and found themselves on a different trail. Realizing they were disoriented, Janie decided to keep the group moving, hoping to find Doug or a way out of the backcountry.

QUESTIONS

1. Good judgment and decision making characterize effective outdoor leaders. What issues associated with judgment and decision making led to this misadventure?

2. What are some of the potential problems or risks involved when splitting one large group into two?

3. Put yourself in Doug and Janie's shoes. What would you have done differently? Explain your answer.

4. An emergency action plan (EAP) is a set of procedures developed to guide an organization's response to an emergency situation. Based on the limited information in this scenario, how would you describe RMS's EAP (good, mediocre, poor, or nonexistent)? Explain your answer.

5. What are some things that might improve RMS's EAP?

6. What resources are required in the event of an emergency? Identify these resources using one of the areas your program uses on a regular basis to conduct programs.

7. What scenarios might activate your program's emergency action plan?

8. When should the families of program participants be notified? When should the local sheriff, local law enforcement personnel, or search and rescue personnel be notified?

Staying on Schedule

Hiro, Chuck, and their crew of 10 students planned to ascend Mount Mitchell, the highest peak in the Eastern United States. Their planned route took them up the Colbert Ridge Trail to the Deep Gap Trail Shelter, where they planned to spend the night. The next day they would backpack along the Black Mountain Crest Trail and complete their trip in Mount Mitchell State Park (MMSP). The trail is rated *very strenuous* because of the constant traversing of all the 6,000-foot+ (1,839 m) peaks along the Black Mountain Ridge and involves some scrambling and steep ascents and descents on a narrow trail tread.

Claudia (a student) was having a difficult time with the demanding hike (the Colbert Ridge Trail gains 2,918 ft over 3.9 mi, or 889 m over 6.3 km). She kept complaining about her 50-pound (22.7 kg) pack and a consistent nagging pain in her left hamstring. Her crewmates helped her throughout the day by taking some of the weight from her pack and urging her on.

It ended up being a long day. When the novice hikers arrived at the shelter, they were exhausted. Claudia continued to complain about the pain in her hamstring. The evening passed without incident. The following morning the students were anxious to get started because they knew that this would be their last day of backpacking and the beginning of a two-day whitewater rafting experience.

The crew got an early start. Approximately one-half mile (0.8 km) from camp, Claudia collapsed, writhing in pain. Evidently, her hamstring had "given out," and she could not walk. Hiro and Chuck assessed the situation and decided that this was a perfect teachable moment. They would have the group construct a litter out of the 100-foot (30.5 m) expedition rope (retired climbing rope) they carried. Once the litter was built and tested, Claudia would be placed in it and carried until she felt better.

The crew did a good job building the litter and within an hour were carrying Claudia down the trail toward MMSP, where they would be met by a resupply vehicle to travel to the river. The carry was very difficult, but going well until Connor, one of the litter bearers at Claudia's head, tripped and fell, striking his head on hers. This knocked Claudia unconscious and caused Connor to "see stars."

What started as a litter exercise now became an emergency. Head trauma can become serious, and both Claudia and Connor presented problems associated with head trauma that put them at risk. The leaders decided that Chuck would run ahead to MMSP to request medical and rescue assistance and contact their course director to let him know their situation. Hiro would remain behind and manage the scene.

A couple of hours later, Chuck returned to the group with a Stokes basket. A plan had been developed at MMSP to carry Claudia in the Stokes basket to the Big Tom Gap Trail and descend to the Maple Camp Bald Trail, where they would meet a four-wheel-drive vehicle (4WD) from the local rescue squad. The 4WD would transport Claudia to the MMSP parking lot, where she would be transferred to an ambulance. The arriving course director would accompany her to the local hospital. Luckily, Connor was able to walk with some assistance.

The all-day litter carry with the Stokes basket went without incident. The group was able to carry Claudia along the demanding terrain to the rendezvous with the 4WD vehicle at approximately 12:30 a.m. Once Claudia was en route, the group continued on to the MMSP parking lot, arriving at approximately 2:00 a.m. to meet their resupply.

Once the gear and exhausted students were loaded, the group departed for the Chattooga River to begin the rafting segment of their course, arriving at approximately 6:00 a.m. Despite the previous day's events, they were able to stay on schedule and meet their river guides at the put-in at around 7:00 a.m. They spent the rest of the day on the river.

QUESTIONS

1. What objective, subjective, and leadership factors can you identify that led to this misadventure?

2. Define *teachable moment*. How would, or should, you use teachable moments in the field? What role does risk management play in identifying and implementing a teachable moment?

3. What are some risk management issues that may arise as a result of trying to stick to a trip's original schedule?

4. How would you and your co-instructor handle this situation? Pair up with another member in your group and discuss your options. Be prepared to present your solution to the rest of your group.

5. Do you anticipate any problems on the river in this scenario? Explain your answer.

Solo Instructing

It was early March and getting near the end of the winter outdoor program season at Outdoors New Hampshire (ONH). Adam was looking forward to leaving New Hampshire and heading south to North Carolina to begin his summer job and be with his fiancée. But before he left, he was contracted to instruct one more wilderness program, a 10-day course with eight male students and Mr. Warren (faculty member) from a prestigious all boys' prep school.

A few days before the course was scheduled to start, Adam met with the ONH program director, who informed him that he was having a difficult time finding a co-instructor. He asked Adam if he would be willing to instruct solo. The program director apologized and told Adam that if he consented to work solo, he would be paid his salary and that of the assistant instructor. Without thinking about the consequences of solo instructing, Adam agreed. After all, it was a short program and the last course of the winter season—what could possibly go wrong?

A couple of days later the group arrived. After a few hours of introductions and packing food and equipment, the group was transported to the Mt. Kinsman Trailhead, where they were to begin their multiday expedition to Mt. Moosilauke. Everyone was in good spirits, with the exception of Greg (a student). Adam noticed that Greg hadn't interacted much with the rest of the group during the equipment and food issue, and he remained quiet during the van ride to the trailhead. He seemed disconnected.

Upon arrival at the trailhead, Adam went over the expedition route noting terrain features, mileage, elevation, campsites, how to walk with and adjust snowshoes, how to put on a pack, and other relevant information. Because it was late in the day, the group would hike approximately 2 miles (3.2 km) to an old Forest Service cabin to spend the night.

About 30 minutes into the hike, Greg broke down and began to cry. He complained about his heavy pack and being tired and cold. He said he missed his family and he didn't want to be out in the woods. He wanted to leave the course. He was adamant. After about an hour of talking and negotiating, Adam decided that there was nothing else he or Mr. Warren could do or say to convince Greg to stay on the hike. There was still some daylight left, and the group was still close to the road, so Adam decided to hike with Greg back to the trailhead and call ONH. Mr. Warren would continue with the group to the cabin. Adam would join them later.

Adam and Greg returned to the trailhead and knocked on the door of the first house they found. The homeowner who answered was familiar with ONH and in fact was an alumna. She agreed to look after Greg until the ONH van returned to pick him up. Adam thanked the homeowner and made his way back up the trail, arriving at the cabin well after dark.

The rest of the evening went on without incident. The following morning the group broke camp and began the climb to the Kinsman Ridge Trail. They continued south along the ridge to Gordon Pond, their next camp. They arrived at Gordon Pond late in the afternoon. Before leaving the trail to head for a campsite along the pond, Adam stopped the group and briefed them on the dangers of crossing ice. He told the group that there was no need to venture out onto the ice and that they should follow the well-marked trail to the campsite.

The group got to the campsite without incident. Some of the students began to set up tents, while others began to dig a kitchen pit and search for firewood. Mr. Warren took this opportunity to walk out onto the pond to take a photograph of the camp. After he had walked approximately 30 feet (9 m) onto the ice, it began to crack. A second later Mr. Warren fell completely through the ice and became fully submerged in the pond. Luckily, one of the students saw him fall through and began shouting for help. Adam, along with five of the students, initiated a successful ice rescue and 30 minutes later had Mr. Warren in dry clothes and a sleeping bag.

QUESTIONS

1. Should solo instructing ever be practiced? Are there any adventure program situations or activities in which solo instructing is practiced? If you answer yes to this question, give examples.

2. What are the appropriate staff/student ratios for conducting various adventure activities?

3. What are the primary risk management issues associated with solo instructing?

4. Crossing lake ice can be a dangerous undertaking during winter adventure activities. What are some accepted practices for crossing ice-covered lakes and ponds in the backcountry?

5. How do you determine whether ice is strong enough to cross?

6. What are some ice rescue techniques that you and your group can implement in the backcountry?

Medical History Can Make a Difference

A group of 10 teenage students (ages 13 to 15) and their two instructors were one week into a two-week backpacking trip in Maine's 100-mile (161 km) wilderness. The weather had been wet most of the first week. This, combined with black flies and mosquitoes, created a significant amount of stress for the students. On the morning of day 8, Rodrigo, one of the students, volunteered to go to the creek to retrieve water for breakfast. When he didn't return in a timely manner, students Amanda and Sue went to look for him. They found him sitting streamside, covered in blood. Amanda ran back to camp to get instructors Bob and Alice and a first aid kit while Sue stayed behind to monitor Rodrigo.

Upon reaching Rodrigo, Bob conducted a patient assessment and discovered that Rodrigo had slit his wrists. First aid was administered and Rodrigo was eventually evacuated to a local hospital, where he recovered from his wounds. His Medical History Form revealed no suicide ideation and no previous visits to a psychiatrist.

During a telephone interview to inform and gather more information, his parents were asked if he had been seeing a psychiatrist for suicide ideation, and they responded, "No never!" After continued questioning by the program director, both parents confessed that they had purposely omitted the suicide information fearing that Rodrigo would not be able to participate in the program and they would not be able to go on their European vacation.

QUESTIONS

1. Why are student and staff medical histories an important risk management tool?

2. What steps does your program take to review student medical histories? Why do you think these are important?

3. How can program leaders verify that the information on a student medical history form is accurate?

4. What legal and ethical obligations do program providers have regarding how the information on a medical history form is used, who it is shared with, and how it is handled and stored?

5. Should a physician be involved in filling out a medical history form? Why do you think this is important?

6. What responsibility do the trip leaders and students have to monitor each other on a trip? Does the responsibility change if a participant has a previous medical history?

7. What information is confidential? Does your workplace have a personal information protection statement that applies to the use of participant information?

Inappropriate Physical Contact

Many adventure programs offer internships to introduce students to their programs' philosophies and operations. Interns are also given opportunities to develop technical and interpersonal skills by working with students in backcountry settings.

Brian (18) was relatively new to the field of outdoor leadership and had the opportunity to work as a summer intern for Outdoor Program Providers (OPP), an environmental education program developed for inner-city youth. As part of his internship, he accompanied groups of students into the backcountry for several days at a time.

During one of these outings, one of the instructors discovered that Brian and a 14-year-old female student had sneaked away from camp one evening for a romantic interlude. When confronted by the instructor, Brian admitted that he and the 14-year-old had spent "about an hour kissing and touching each other."

QUESTIONS

1. What are the risk management issues (if any) associated with this incident?

2. What are the ethical ramifications of this incident? Legal ramifications?

3. Should programs have a policy about boys and girls tenting together? Explain your answer.

4. What action should the instructor take given this situation? What action should the program take?

5. Should the girl's parents be notified?

6. How would you address this situation if you directed this program?

7. Would your reaction be different if the female participant were 18 years old?

8. What is the age of consent in your state?

Waterfall Presents a Danger

The Department of Physical Education at Valley State College offers a series of outdoor pursuits courses for credit. Backpacking, one of the courses offered, includes both classroom instruction and a weekend field trip. A single instructor and 14 students make up the class and participate in the field trip.

During the fall semester the field trip took place in a nearby national forest known for its numerous waterfalls. The group reached the trailhead early on Saturday morning and began the hike, anticipating getting into camp later that afternoon. Just before reaching camp, the group walked by High Falls, one of the primary waterfalls in the area. Several of the students wanted to stop and explore the falls. The instructor suggested that the group proceed to camp; once camp was set up, students who were interested could return and explore the area.

After setting up camp, eight of the students showed an interest in exploring the High Falls area. The instructor agreed to lead the group of eight back to the falls and instructed the remaining six students to stay in camp.

The group hiked approximately 1 mile (1.6 km) back to the base of the 50-foot (15.2 m) waterfall. A couple of students decided to hike to the top of the falls via a side trail. The instructor was reluctant to let the two students go by themselves and suggested that everyone go. All agreed to go except Pete, who said that he would wait at the base of the falls for the group to return. The instructor was reluctant to leave Pete behind and had him promise that he would not leave his spot. Satisfied, the group left Pete napping and started up the steep trail.

The group reached the top of the falls and continued another 100 feet (30.5 m) upstream to cross the stream, planning to descend on the opposite side. As the group began the descent, the instructor was able to look down to the base of the trail and noticed that Pete was not where he was supposed to be. An instant later everyone heard a shout, turned around, and saw Pete butt sliding down the stream toward the lip of the waterfall, and a fall of over 50 feet (15.2 m). Luck was on Pete's side that afternoon. He stopped just before going over the brink when his momentum carried him into a hole carved into the streambed! The entire group ran to his aid. He was rescued when the instructor and another student were able to pull him to the stream bank with a long pole made from a sapling.

QUESTIONS

1. What are the circumstances that led to this potentially lethal situation?

2. What practices could be initiated to prevent another incident like this from happening?

3. What role did leadership play in this misadventure?

4. What is intuition? What role should it play in instructor decision making?

Accidents, Incidents, and Misadventures

Bridge Jumping

Ten students and two staff members from a university scholars program were participating in a five-day multisport program (one full day of travel, one day of rock climbing, and three days of whitewater rafting). The whitewater rafting component was the highlight of the program. The group was able to negotiate the class II-IV river without incident. Approximately 1 mile (1.6 km) before the takeout, an old metal highway bridge appeared. It was situated approximately 20 feet (6 m) above the river. The bridge was no longer in use because a newer, more modern bridge had replaced it.

Seeing the bridge, one of the students asked the lead instructor, Ted, if they could jump off the bridge into the river below. After all, it would be a great way to finish an awesome whitewater rafting trip! Without hesitation, Ted replied "Go for it!" This decision was unacceptable to Nicole, the assistant instructor, who let Ted know that to her the risks involved were unacceptable. Ted disagreed and told Nicole not to worry because students would be wearing their PFDs, and besides, he had personally jumped from the bridge with no problem. The discussion went on for several more minutes, and Nicole reluctantly gave in.

The rafts were beached, and the students climbed up the steep riverbank. One by one they lined up to take their turns jumping off the bridge. Ted and Nicole got into one of the rafts and positioned themselves under the bridge as a "safety boat" and waited. Once they were in position, the students jumped one by one into the river. About halfway through, a number of spectators showed up and began to encourage the students by chanting, "Jump, jump, jump!" One student, Sean, was reluctant to jump, but under both peer and spectator pressure, he did.

As Sean jumped, the back of his head struck the bridge railing rendering him unconscious. He hit the water in a belly flop and began drifting downstream. Luckily, his PFD righted him. Ted and Nicole were able to retrieve him. As they pulled him into the raft, he regained consciousness. One of the spectators called 911. The group was met at the takeout by an ambulance, and Sean was transported to the local hospital. He was kept overnight for observation and was released the following morning.

QUESTIONS

1. Have you ever been in a situation in which you couldn't agree with your co-instructor? What was the outcome? How did you come to a decision?

2. What would you suggest as a program guideline to prevent leader disagreements?

3. Besides the obvious, what are some other underlying risk management issues that this misadventure presents?
4. How can a situation like this be prevented?

Client Injured While Rafting

Ms. Kuo and her daughter were passengers in a raft that was part of a group that included other rafts and boats. Among the other passengers in Ms. Kuo's raft was a guide who was an employee of the raft company. During the trip, a participant fell out of a kayak and Ms. Kuo's raft was directed to the riverbank by the guide, who got out with a throw rope. The guide tossed one end of the rope to the participant in the river. Rather than grabbing the throw rope, the participant swam toward the raft and grabbed it, which caused another passenger in the raft to fall into the water. At this point the guide threw the entire rope into Ms. Kuo's raft.

One end of the rope became caught under the water, and the other end wrapped around Ms. Kuo's lower right leg and began crushing it. Ms. Kuo shouted to the guide to cut the rope with a knife to free her leg, but the guide replied that he did not have a knife. He shouted to the senior guide and the other guides to bring him a knife, but no one had one.

At this point the guide in Ms. Kuo's raft froze and did nothing. Ms. Kuo asked him to jump into the river to try to free the rope. He was able to create enough slack on the rope that it could be removed from Ms. Kuo's leg.

Eventually the guides were able to move Ms. Kuo to shore where she was in excruciating pain and suffering from respiratory and circulatory problems. The guides did not have communication equipment with them so they could not contact outside sources for help. One of the guides ran to a road to locate a telephone and call for help. After three hours, Ms. Kuo was transported to a hospital.

Once at home, Ms. Kuo was seen by a vascular surgeon and other physicians, who diagnosed a strangulation injury to her lower right leg. In addition, her physicians referred her for psychological treatment.

QUESTIONS

1. Are there established methods, techniques, standards, or practices that could have been implemented to prevent this accident?

2. What standard emergency and rescue equipment should be carried on every commercial or private raft trip?

3. What would you use in the absence of communication equipment?

4. What is negligence? What factors are necessary for proving negligence? Were factors present in this misadventure to consider negligence? If so, what were they?

5. The most important way to defeat a negligence claim is to show that one or more of the four elements of negligence have not been met. Investigate the legal literature and identify the *defenses to negligence* that may be used to defeat a negligence claim.

Summit Attempt

Perry is a progressive private residential high school in the northwestern United States. Like many private schools in the region, it offers a variety of academic, athletic, and extracurricular activities. Tradition also plays an important role in the Perry experience. During the spring semester, Perry seniors are required to participate in a five-day Ridge Trail Traverse that culminates with a summit attempt on the region's highest peak. Perry seniors prepare for this experience by taking part in a number of outdoor skills courses offered by interested faculty, and by camping on select weekends throughout their four years as students.

During March 2007, a group of 15 Perry seniors, one parent, two teachers, and two experienced mountain guides began their journey. Local weather reported that trail conditions were marginal and that a cold front was approaching. Clouds covered the ridges with temperatures in the mid 30s (F; approximately 1.7 °C), intermittent rain and snow, and winds of 25 to 30 miles per hour (40 to 48 km/h).

Their route started on the Summit Ridge Trail. Within the first three hours of the climb, five students and the one parent turned back because of fatigue and wetness. Three hours later, one of the guides aggravated an old back injury and also turned back. The group continued climbing in deteriorating weather conditions and reached tree line. One of the teachers made the decision to continue after the storm began, telling the group that no Perry group had ever turned back. The group reached the gap between Mt. Harding and Mt. Wilson by late afternoon. By now it was snowing heavily, and the temperature had dropped to 20 °F (−6.7 °C). At this point the group decided to turn back.

While making their descent, the group got caught in a whiteout, decided they could go no farther, and began to set up their tents. Unfortunately, the five students and parent who had turned back earlier took essential gear with them including tent poles. There was nothing they could do except to sit on their sleeping pads and cover themselves with their sleeping bags and tents and huddle together under a rock overhang to wait out the storm. The three stoves they had were useless in the high winds. Several attempts were made to build quinzees (shelters made by hollowing out a pile of settled snow) for shelter, but there wasn't enough snow and they had only one shovel. People were getting wet and cold.

The next morning it was snowing heavily, with the wind gusting up to 35 miles per hour (56 km/h). Two students and the remaining guide left the group and hiked down the mountain for several hours to get help. They reached the highway and were able to flag down a snowplow. The snowplow driver contacted the state fish and game department, which initiated a rescue.

Freezing and snowy weather comes with its own set of risks, in addition to the ones organizations must worry about during dry and warm weather. What are these risks, and how can an organization prepare participants and guides?

Photo courtesy Aram Attarian.

One full day after an extensive air and ground search, rescuers finally located the overhang and found the remaining students and staff buried under 4 feet (1.2 m) of snow.

Miraculously, three of the students were alive. Five students and the two teachers were dead.

QUESTIONS

1. What role did leadership play in this tragedy?

2. What hazardous attitudes were involved in this incident?

3. What were the primary factors contributing to this tragedy? Review table 1.1 and categorize the primary factors you identify into unsafe acts, unsafe conditions, and errors in judgment.

4. What is the right balance between expected gains and anticipated risks? Does it ever make sense to put a group into real risk situations? Explain your answer.

5. How does trying to survive as a group differ from trying to survive alone?

6. When contracting with guides and outfitters, who has the final say in decision making, especially when lives are at stake—the guides or the program provider (in this case, the Perry School)? Explain your answer.

Outing Turns Tragic

A teenage girl is dead after a tragic rappelling accident over the weekend. Madison Baker, 15, was one of a group of local youth on a church outing in Old Ford National Forest. The group was led by youth pastor and former U.S. Navy SEAL Zach Parks, who has been taking groups on the same outing for the past 11 years.

Witnesses stated that Baker and another teen were rappelling in "Swiss seat" harnesses using two ropes when Baker began free-falling. It was later determined that Baker's rope, which was secured to a boulder at the top of the cliff, had come loose. Baker struck the edge of the ledge partway down the cliff where her climbing partner was resting before descending another 40 feet (12 m) to a lake at the bottom of the cliff. One of the other teens in the group waiting to rappel was able to call 911 on his cell phone, summoning paramedics to the scene.

Parks pulled Baker from the lake and administered CPR, but the girl was unresponsive. She was pronounced dead at the scene by the county medical examiner; preliminary autopsy results indicated that the cause of death was brain hemorrhaging.

While trying to reach Baker, Parks fell about 15 feet (4.6 m) cracking five ribs and receiving scalp lacerations. While he was being treated for these injuries, it was discovered that he also had a collapsed lung.

Senior pastor Rev. James Dickerson spoke to reporters outside the Baker home. "As a community we are devastated by the loss of Madison. Pastor Zach has led these outings for years to the same location without incident. We ask for your prayers and support for Madison's parents during this very difficult time."

QUESTIONS

1. What factors (equipment, technique, instruction, standards) contributed to this accident? How would you describe the site in terms of appropriateness for this activity? Explain your answer.

2. If you had to use this site for a rappelling experience with your own group, what would you do to prevent an incident like this?

3. Should land management agencies such as the U.S. Forest Service require group leaders to possess a certain level of training or certification to bring climbing groups on their lands? Explain your answer.

Injury on the Challenge Course

Keydra Rhoades, a middle-aged patient, entered Get Better Hospital (GBH) as part of a drug intervention program. Several days after her admission, she was scheduled to participate in a series of low ropes course events (or team-building activities). One event, Walking-the-Line, involved holding a fixed rope for balance and walking on a cable stretched between two trees. The object was for other patients to catch any person who fell, thereby instilling trust among group members. Keydra did not want to participate in the activities because she was not physically active, and she expressed her reservations to Sheila, the instructor facilitating the activities. Keydra also shared her reservations with another student her age as well as with a younger patient with hip problems.

Before the activities began, Sheila had the group warm up with an aerobic activity. As soon as the warm-up began, Keydra fell, striking her right knee on the ground. She let Sheila know about the incident, and Sheila let Keydra sit out the rest of the warm-up. While limping to the team-building course, Keydra again expressed concern about participating. Sheila asked her to try and assured her that if she fell, the group would catch her.

Keydra watched the entire group successfully complete the Walking-the-Line event. She was the last to go. When it was her turn, she was about 4 feet (1.2 m) from the first tree when she fell. The group was not able to catch her, and she landed on her right knee. Keydra was taken by ambulance to the emergency room at the local hospital where she was diagnosed with a dislocated kneecap. Two weeks later Keydra sued GBH.

QUESTIONS

1. What circumstances led to Keydra's injury?

2. Is there an established method, technique, or practice that could have prevented this accident?

3. What is the difference between general and specific supervision? Based on this situation, which type of supervision would have been more appropriate?

4. What are some ethical guidelines for facilitators?

5. What is the facilitator's role in safety prior to the program, at the beginning of the program, during the program, and after the program?

Day Hike Turns Into Overnight

On December 2, 2000, a group of four staff members and two students from a New England school left the Lafayette Campground parking lot at 7:30 a.m., intending to do the popular loop hike up the Falling Waters Trail, across the Franconia Ridge to Mt. Lafayette, then down the Greenleaf Trail and Old Bridle Path to the starting point.

The staff members included Rob (the leader), Mary, Susan, and Joe. The students were a 15-year-old girl and a 13-year-old boy. Rob carried a compass, but his only map was one he had traced, which included only the route he intended to take.

There was new snow on the ground from the start, increasing to about a foot at tree-line, but, except for Rob, none of the others had the appropriate footwear for the conditions with temperatures below freezing, and their other clothing was minimal. They carried headlamps, but not a stove or any other camping gear, except for a three-person bivy sack. As they ascended, they passed a pair of hikers who noticed that the boy was hiking in GORE-TEX sneakers with his arms wrapped around his chest as if he were cold. They offered him a pair of neoprene socks but he refused the offer. These two hikers were putting on their above tree-line gear when Mary, who had decided not to continue passed them on her descent. (The two hikers were well equipped, but decided to turn back, because one of them did not have goggles and they felt it was too risky to continue without them.) Mary reported that Rob had done this hike several times and said "It's a ridge; you can't get lost."

At the summit of Little Haystack, when Mary decided to turn back because of the cold temperatures, high winds, and poor visibility due to blowing snow, two other members of the group were cold and also thinking of turning back, but another co-leader gave them more clothes, and they decided to continue. According to the group, the question of any danger in continuing was not mentioned. They lost the trail in whiteout conditions before reaching the summit of Mt. Lafayette and found themselves on the east side of the summit cone. It is very possible they ended up on one of the several knobs north of Lafayette and mistook it for the summit. Since the leader was unfamiliar with the trails and had no useful map, they kept hiking without proper direction, missing trails that would have led them down to safety. They continued hiking until about 8:30 p.m. and probably reached the vicinity of Hellgate Brook, where they decided to bivouac (a temporary camp without tent or other cover). Luckily the leader had a cigarette lighter and they were able to build a fire. Two students and one adult were able to crawl into the bivy sack. It was a cold night, undoubtedly well below freezing. They did not know that only another two to three hours of hiking would have brought them down to the Kancamagus Highway and safety.

The next day they retraced their entire route up to the ridge and over Mt. Garfield to the summit of Mt. Lafayette, again passing trails that would have led them down to the trailhead. Fortunately, this time they did find the Greenleaf Trail and descended, reaching the parking lot at 4:35 p.m.

Reprinted, by permission, from Appalachia Mountain Club, 2001, "Day hike turns into overnight," *Appalachia* 115-117.

QUESTIONS

1. What knowledge and experience level are required to lead a group in an activity?

2. What equipment and clothing would be needed for a winter day hike to a mountain summit?

3. What kind of policy statement would address this situation?

4. Did this group have a trip plan? Explain.

5. What information should be included in a trip plan?

6. How might better pretrip planning have prevented this situation?

7. If a participant registers and pays for an institutional winter hiking trip and doesn't have the proper clothing, should that person be allowed to participate on the trip? Explain your answer.

Training Exercise Goes Wrong

On March 15, 2003, Randy Jones (22) was participating in a rappel training exercise near one of the access gullies, west of the Amphitheatre in Pilot Mountain State Park. He was with a group of EMS/firefighters from a local community college when he fell to the ground below.

The instructor, Bill Snyder, a witness to the accident, stated that the group of ten students had just completed the instructional section of their training when Randy was beginning to rappel. According to Snyder, Randy "panicked" as he went over the cliff edge, lost control, and fell approximately 40 feet (12 m) to the rocks below, landing head-first.

Two members of the group went to the parking lot, a short distance away to call 911. Since most of the participants in the group were EMTs or paramedics, first aid was started immediately. Randy was semi-conscious throughout the incident and was described as "combative" by rescue personnel. Even though he was wearing a helmet, the length of the fall combined with his body weight of 240 lbs caused his helmet to collapse, resulting in a severe skull fracture. He was evacuated through a high angle rescue and transported via helicopter to the local medical center.

Reprinted, by permission, from J.E. Williamson, 2007, *Accidents in North American Mountaineering* (Hanover, NH).

QUESTIONS

1. What is the role and responsibility of the group leader in a situation such as this?

2. What are some fundamental risk management practices that were ignored?

3. What are the standard operating procedures for conducting this rappelling exercise?

Demonstration Goes Wrong

On September 21, Jake Morgan (28), Wilderness Academy School administrator and climbing guide, fell to his death while teaching a beginning rescue class. The school, composed of teachers and students in grades 7-12, were completing the rescue course in preparation for their five-week trip to Alaska when the accident occurred.

Jake had just completed a demonstration on the safety of a two-point load distributing anchor system. He had two anchor points and a webbing loop joining the two in the approved configuration. He was attached directly from his harness to the load-distributing webbing loop with a carabiner.

Morgan would normally cut the webbing runner between the anchor and the carabiner connecting it to the load distributing webbing loop to demonstrate how the second anchor point will "catch" the load if the first anchor point fails. However, for some unknown reason, he actually cut the load distributing webbing loop instead. Since this was a loop and the system was under load, Morgan was unable to catch himself before the cut loop ran through his main attachment carabiner. He subsequently fell to his death.

Reprinted, by permission, from J.E. Williamson, 1997, *Accidents in North American Mountaineering* (Hanover, NH), 29.

QUESTIONS

1. What is edge behavior? How did it contribute to this accident?

2. What are the dangers of using a knife around a loaded rope or webbing? What are the alternatives?

3. How would you demonstrate a load-distributing anchor without putting yourself at risk? Explain in detail.

4. How would this situation have been different with the appropriate safety precautions? Reconstruct the scenario.

Lost Kayakers

On September 12, 2005, a group of students from the Green School accompanied by teachers Russell and Karima set out from Flamingo, Florida, and headed southwest, over the open water of Florida Bay on a 7-mile (11.3 km) paddle to Carl Ross Key, where they planned to camp for the night. The pod consisted of sea kayaks and a motorized pontoon boat piloted by Karima. During the paddle, the pod became separated, partly as a result of the inexperience of the paddlers and 1- to 2-foot (30 to 60 cm) seas.

As the pontoon boat neared Carl Ross Key, Karima began circling back to try to gather the boats that were lagging behind. At dusk, the boat's motor quit, and no matter how hard Karima tried, she couldn't restart the engine. By this time all of the kayaks, with the exception of one containing two of the boys, were accounted for. As it became dark, it started to rain, the wind increased, and 2- to 3-foot (60 to 90 cm) waves developed.

Around 9 p.m., the group spotted a light in the distance. Thinking it might be a signal from the two boys, Russell and Stan (a student), got into one of the kayaks to investigate. About 20 minutes later, the pair became disoriented and could no longer see the light. They continued to paddle for one to two hours toward what they thought were lights somewhere on Cape Sable. At this point, Russell decided to stop and use his cell phone. He was able to call his wife in Jacksonville, who in turn called Everglades National Park (ENP). ENP requested air support from the Coast Guard, who eventually located the group of kayakers still tied up to the drifting pontoon boat around 3:00 a.m. An ENP boat brought them to park headquarters.

At 4:00 a.m. the Coast Guard helicopter located and hoisted the kayak with Russell and Stan who had never rejoined the larger group. The search continued for the two boys in the missing kayak. Rescuers searched a 50-mile (80 km) area in grid patterns through the night and weekend. The two boys were found dead in the water near Roscoe Key on Monday afternoon.

QUESTIONS

1. What objective and subjective factors contributed to this tragedy?
2. How would you describe the skill level of Russell and Karima and of the students? How did skill level contribute to this tragedy?
3. What are some things you would do differently to prevent a tragedy like this?

4. What is an emergency action plan (EAP)? Do you believe the Green School had one? If your answer is no, create an outline identifying the important components of an EAP for the Green School.

5. What safety and emergency equipment should be available on sea kayaking trips?

6. Create a Haddon matrix to address the potential risks associated with sea kayaking.

7. In a group of three or four, create a float plan, or curriculum, that uses a stepping-stone approach to teach sea kayaking to beginners.

Instructors Charged With Murder

Six outdoor program instructors were charged with murder in the death of Parker Yeats (13), who was restrained for over an hour at the Wilderness Camp for Wayward Youth (WCWY). Yeats was on probation after being charged with arson and was voluntarily attending the wilderness program.

A grand jury deliberated for about an hour before returning the charges of felony murder, child cruelty, and involuntary manslaughter. Yeats died the day after he was held facedown by counselors at WCWY. Investigation into his death revealed that Parker, who had asthma, was denied his inhaler during the restraint.

Parker was restrained by at least three counselors after he confronted one of them for denying him food as punishment. He eventually stopped breathing. An attorney for one of the instructors said that the instructors restrained Parker as they had been trained to do. However, a WCWY program director said the instructors were not following program rules or procedures, noting that the program does not train its staff to do facedown restraints. The program has retrained staff on the use of restraints since the incident and is reviewing its policies on when restraint may be used.

QUESTIONS

1. What are some of the operational differences that distinguish recreation- and education-based outdoor adventure programs from therapeutic outdoor programs or from commercial guiding businesses?

2. What are some of the risk management and safety challenges of working with adjudicated youth?

3. Investigate the use of restraints in adaptive outdoor adventure programs. When are restraints appropriate? What types are permissible?

4. What other options can programs implement to address uncooperative or belligerent participants?

Chapter 4

Environmental Conditions

Adventure programs and guided activities are conducted in unique natural environments that expose participants to risks that must be managed. In their book *Hazards in Mountaineering and How to Avoid Them*, Paulcke and Dumler (1976) described the risk factors associated with natural settings as objective, or environmental, hazards. Guides and outdoor leaders have very little control over these "acts of God." Some of the more common hazards encountered in outdoor program environments are weather, interactions with wildlife, stream and river crossings, icy roads, and the many hazards associated with traveling in mountainous terrain.

• *Weather*—Weather plays an important role in the conduct and outcome of adventure activities by changing conditions in the environment. Weather includes precipitation, wind, and temperature.

   • *Precipitation*—Precipitation in its various forms (e.g., rain, snow, hail), or a lack thereof, can introduce additional stress into a program and create problems with transportation, river levels, and potable water; it can also cause property damage. Thunderstorms can pose multiple dangers to program participants, especially when they involve heavy rain, hail, and lightning.

   • *Wind*—High winds can blow climbers off their feet at a summit, cause climbers to abandon a climb, and keep canoeists and sea kayakers in camp. Gusts of wind can damage tents and increase the threat of hypothermia. Blowing snow can create whiteouts, which can result in navigation and other safety problems.

   • *Temperature*—Ambient temperature plays an important role in program safety. When it is too hot, the potential for heat-related illnesses increases; when it is too cold, hypothermia, frostbite, and other cold-related injuries become a concern. Wearing clothing appropriate for the environment, staying hydrated, eating well, and monitoring physical activity can protect people from temperature extremes.

• *Lightning*—Lightning is a potential objective hazard in almost all outdoor program environments. Most outdoor adventure programs in the United States and Canada conduct activities throughout the year, although the majority take place from March through October. As expected, almost all (92 percent) of the lightning-related casualties in the United States occur between the months of May and September, with a peak in July (Adekoya & Nolte, 2005). Lightning is a clear and present objective danger recognized by providers of outdoor adventure programs. Those responsible for conducting these activities assume a special responsibility to ensure that adequate precautions are taken to prevent accidents.

• *Interactions with wildlife*—Guided and adventure programs operate in settings where human–wildlife encounters are becoming more commonplace. These encounters can lead to interactions that result in injury to both wildlife and people. Human–wildlife interactions include wildlife conflicts with people, as well as people harassing or in other ways negatively interacting with wildlife. Human activity can affect wildlife by permanently changing the physical environment or altering animal behavior (Steidl & Powell, 2006). For example, a poorly maintained backcountry campsite can attract bears and other wildlife looking for food. Instructors or guides who conduct activities in bear or cougar country need to be educated and prepared to deal with these potentially deadly animals. Other problems associated with wildlife include contracting rabies and being stung (e.g., by bees, wasps, spiders, scorpions, or marine invertebrates) or bit (e.g., by snakes).

Stream and river crossings are a common risk factor for hikers. What are some things an organization can do to prepare for this risk?

Photo courtesy of Keith Crawford.

• *Lake, river, and stream crossings*—Crossing rivers, streams, and frozen lakes are some of the most dangerous activities undertaken in backcountry travel. Moving water creates problems such as foot entrapments, strainers, and being swept over drops and waterfalls. Strainers are formed when an object like a tree blocks the passage of larger objects (for example, a canoe or kayak) but allows the flow of water to continue. A drop forms on the downstream side of a ledge. The term *waterfall* is reserved for ledges that form drops over 10 feet (3 m) high. Crossing frozen lakes and streams in winter creates an additional set of challenges. Guides and outdoor leaders need to familiarize themselves with safe stream-crossing techniques, develop skills at reading water, and understand stream dynamics to increase the margin of safety.

• *Rock fall*—Rock fall is an objective hazard common in mountainous terrain that can be caused by other climbers, heavy precipitation, and the action of freezing and thawing. Climbers can minimize the danger of rock fall through good route finding, hazard assessment, and careful climbing (e.g., testing handholds and learning how to recognize the signs of previous rock falls).

• *Avalanche*—Avalanche is one of the most underestimated objective dangers in the backcountry. According to the Colorado Avalanche Information Center (2011), 23 avalanche fatalities were recorded in the United States during winter 2010-2011. Many traveling in avalanche terrain generally think that they will be able to recognize the hazards of avalanche and survive being caught. Avalanches usually occur on long, wide-open, 30- to 45-degree slopes with few trees or large rocks. Ninety percent of reported victims are caught in avalanches triggered by themselves or others in their group. New snow following a large storm and solar radiation can trigger an avalanche. Wind, precipitation, and temperature also play important roles in avalanche potential (American Institute for Avalanche Research and Education, 2011a).

"The sole protection against objective hazards (e.g., avalanche) is the observation and understanding of these natural phenomena" (Paulcke & Dumler, 1976, pg. 11). All guides and instructors of activities that occur in avalanche terrain should be trained in avalanche awareness. The American Institute for Avalanche Research and Education (2011b) offers an avalanche awareness program targeting the young and unaware backcountry user. This one- to two-hour program teaches participants how to recognize avalanche danger and reduce the risk. They learn (1) where and why avalanches occur, (2) who gets caught and why, and (3) a basic approach to staying safe in the backcountry. Advanced courses for instructors and guides teach decision making in avalanche terrain (level 1), teach how to analyze snow stability and avalanche hazard (level 2), and provide advanced avalanche training for professional and recreation leaders (level 3).

MINIMIZING OBJECTIVE DANGERS

Environmental, or objective, risks can be minimized by being aware of the hazards (education), modifying behavior, and being prepared in the event that a problem occurs. The best protection against these hazards is an understanding of the risk and careful observation, combined with appropriate equipment, clothing, and tactics. For example, programs should have well-developed lightning safety plans that include information on the physics of lightning, the warning signs of lightning, areas to avoid in the event of a thunderstorm, actions to take when caught in a thunderstorm, information specific to the outdoor activity offered (e.g., hiking, rock climbing, water-based activities), first aid treatment, and the misconceptions surrounding lightning.

SUMMARY

Guided and adventure program providers have limited control over objective, or environmental, hazards. The best protection comes from experience and learning as much as possible about these natural phenomena combined with appropriate equipment, skill, and tactics. Weather, interactions with wildlife, stream and river crossings, rock fall, and avalanche are some of the more common objective hazards encountered while conducting adventure activities. The scenarios that follow highlight some common objective hazards (e.g., weather, wildlife, moving water, terrain) that outdoor leaders may encounter in the backcountry settings in which they work.

Scout Leaders Say They Got No Warning

Leaders of a North Carolina Boy Scout troop and Virginia State Park rangers disagree about whether the troop was warned that dangerous weather threatened the park where the scouts held their annual camping trip last weekend. Eleven Scouts and leaders of troop 11 had to be rescued Sunday from Grayson Highlands State Park, just across the Virginia line from the northwest corner of North Carolina. All were treated for frostbite and hypothermia, and six spent the night at Ashe Memorial Hospital in Jefferson, NC. The Scout leader said no one warned of the blizzard-like conditions to come. But two rangers at Grayson Highlands State Park said they told Scout leaders that a cold front would sling sleet, snow, rain, and wind gusts across the mountains.

Reprinted by permission of *The News & Observer of Raleigh, NC.*

QUESTIONS

1. Whose responsibility is it to check the weather report before departing on an outing? Explain your answer.
2. What are six sources of weather information you can access before departing on an outing in your area?
3. What type of weather will usually cancel a trip? What factors will you use to determine whether to continue a trip in the case of problematic weather?
4. What are the signs and symptoms of hypothermia? Frostbite?
5. What are the four mechanisms for heat loss? How can each of these be managed through appropriate clothing, equipment, and monitoring physical activity?

Lightning Strikes Climbers

A 26-year-old climber was killed by lightning Saturday during a thunderstorm while rock climbing at Hanging Rock State Park, NC. He was pronounced dead at Stokes-Reynolds Memorial Hospital at Danbury, authorities said. He and several friends were climbing when a thunderstorm began, authorities said. The group sought shelter under a ledge and lightning hit the mountain early Saturday afternoon.

QUESTIONS

1. What are various ways hikers, climbers, and other outdoor enthusiasts can be struck by lightning?

2. What was the climber doing in this scenario to expose himself to a lightning strike?

3. What would you do if you were caught midclimb during a thunderstorm? Provide several options.

4. What are some misconceptions or myths about lightning? Share them with the rest of your group.

5. What is the difference between high-risk and low-risk environments in terms of lightning safety?

Lightning Strikes Campers

According to reports, over a dozen campers from Camp Zeus were struck by ground current associated with a nearby lightning strike. Most of the campers suffered entry and exit burns. There were no fatalities. The group was on an overnight outing on camp property when a late-afternoon thunderstorm moved in. According to camp director Daniel Baugh, lightning struck within 10 feet (3 m) of the group's Adirondack-style shelters.

Campers were lying on their sleeping bags when lightning struck, and most received burns where their bodies came in contact with the ground. Mollie Drager, one of the counselors accompanying the group of 12- and 13-year-olds, said that one of the campers was lying on his back with his head resting on one of the camp's dogs when lightning struck. The boy received burns on his head and neck. The electrical current killed the dog.

QUESTIONS

1. What are the high-risk environments in this scenario related to lightning safety?
2. Are tents, tarps, or trail shelters safe places during a thunderstorm? Explain your answer.
3. What is the lightning position?
4. As leader of this group, what would you have done to create a low-risk environment in this situation?

Man Struck by Lightning on Solo Hike

Park rangers received a cell phone call around 11:00 a.m. that John Doe (31) was injured on Longs Peak. Other hikers in "The Narrows" area close to the junction had found him in "The Homestretch" at roughly 13,800 feet (4,206.2 m). The initial reports indicated that he had hiked to Longs Peak the day before and had spent an unplanned night in the backcountry. With cloud-to-cloud lightning all around him, Doe took shelter under a rock outcropping to wait for the stormy weather to pass. Then, he blacked out. He regained consciousness some time later and was able to walk slowly with assistance but was unable to recall what had caused his injuries. Continued phone calls to park dispatch by visitors along the route, indicated that visitors were assisting the man down the route. They were also providing dry clothing, food, and water. A park trail crew in the area reached the man and determined that Doe had been struck by lightning sometime the day before. Doe had numerous burn injuries.

The trail crew was able to provide immediate care and continued to walk him to the Agnes Vaille shelter, a primitive historic shelter, located at "The Keyhole." They waited out an intense storm with lightning, hail, heavy rains, and low temperatures. Once the severe storm passed, they began walking slowly down the route and connected with park rangers at "The Boulderfield." Rangers provided more emergency medical care to the man.

The first litter team of park staff reached the patient in late afternoon. Due to the severe weather in the area during the beginning of the rescue, helicopters were unable to fly. Weather conditions improved and at approximately 6:30 p.m. Flight for Life flew the patient to St. Anthony Central.

Doe, a college student, was visiting Rocky Mountain National Park with a group of students as part of a field study on climate change. He ignored the advice of his instructor and attempted to summit Longs Peak, alone.

Adapted from K. Patterson. Available: http://www.nps.gov/romo/parknews/pr_lightning_strike.htm.

QUESTIONS

1. What dangers are associated with hiking solo?
2. What equipment should a solo hiker or climber carry when attempting a summit? What equipment should a group carry when attempting a summit?

Having a plan in place for what to do during lightning can save lives. What should you do during an electrical storm if you are hiking, rock climbing, or whitewater rafting?

iStockphoto.com/Chris Hobbs

3. Research to discover what the term *turnaround time* means in relation to lightning? What is the turnaround time for the Rocky Mountain region? Why is this an important consideration when participating in outdoor activities during the summer?

4. What is the 30/30 rule?

5. What is your program's lightning safety protocol? If your program does not have a lightning safety protocol, create one.

Excessive Heat Can Kill

When the body becomes overheated, heat-related illnesses can occur, including dehydration, heat cramps, heat exhaustion, and heatstroke. Heat-related deaths occur each summer in the desert.

Bruce Holliday (16), a participant in an Arizona-based wilderness program, died after backpacking in temperatures exceeding 98 °F (36.7 °C). Bruce, along with six other students and two instructors, was on a 10-day backpacking trip in Arizona's Chihuahuan Desert. The group was completing a 5-mile (8 km) hike on day 3 of the program when Bruce began complaining about being dizzy and experiencing muscle cramps. The group stopped, and the instructors made sure Bruce had plenty to drink. His condition did not improve. He began vomiting, causing both instructors to become concerned. They assessed Bruce and noted a drop on the AVPU (alert, voice, pain, unresponsive) scale and hot, red, and dry skin. They began to treat him for heatstroke by moving him into the shade and requested an immediate evacuation via a cell phone call to their base of operations. Bruce died while being transported to the hospital. An autopsy revealed that his death was heat related.

QUESTIONS

1. What protocols should adventure programs have for managing activities on extremely hot days?

2. What are the definitions of dehydration, heat cramps, heat exhaustion, and heatstroke?

3. What are some proactive practices to undertake to prevent heat-related problems from happening to you or a member of your group?

4. Does your program have a protocol in place to address adventure activities on hot days? If not, create one.

Avalanche Kills Skiers

Six college students were killed in an avalanche in the French Alps. The group (10 students and two guides) was spending the winter break in Chamonix cross-country skiing. Both guides were experienced skiers and had received AIRE Level 2 avalanche training (i.e., a four-day program that teaches guides and backcountry instructors how to analyze snow stability and avalanche hazard). Avalanches are common in the area, and the avalanche danger at the time was "considerable" (i.e., natural avalanches are possible, and human-triggered avalanches are probable), although the area was not off-limits to skiing.

The six survivors were taken to safety by helicopter. Two were admitted to the hospital, and others suffered minor injuries. The avalanche ran for about a half a mile (0.8 km), burying some victims under 8 feet (2.4 m) of snow.

QUESTIONS

1. In your opinion, what were the contributing factors to this tragic accident?

2. Can tragedies of this type be avoided? Explain your answer.

3. What conditions cause avalanches? What should you do if you are caught in an avalanche?

4. The chances of a buried victim being found alive and rescued are higher when everyone in a group is carrying standard avalanche equipment and has been trained in how to use it. What personal equipment should people carry in avalanche terrain to increase the chances of being found if they are buried? List each item and explain its use.

5. What is the Avalanche Danger Scale? How can this be used as a decision-making tool?

6. What are some proactive measures you and your group can take when traveling in avalanche terrain? Create a Haddon matrix to organize your response.

Mountain Lion Stalks Group

Two guides and eight clients from the Northwest Explorers Club were participating in a multiday sea kayaking course on northeastern Vancouver Island, British Columbia. The area is known for its heavily forested islands, scenery, and abundant wildlife. The group was supported by a powerboat to be used only in the case of an emergency. It could be on site within an hour.

The first few days went according to schedule. Clients were working well together, and according to the instructors, "were getting a lot out of the course." Early in the afternoon on day 5, the group made camp on a remote Vancouver Island beach. Tents were set up, a cook area was established, and a waste and toilet area identified.

Around 3:00 p.m., Melissa and Linda, both clients, decided to walk along the beach. The women hadn't traveled far from camp when a mountain lion sprang out of cover, bounded up to them, and crouched low just a few feet away. Both women screamed and threw a piece of driftwood at the cat causing it to run back into the woods. The women ran back to camp and reported the encounter to the guides, Tim and Jan. They were surprised to hear the women's story and told the group not to worry, given that they were a large group and that this in itself would keep the lion at bay. Unknown to both guides and clients, mountain lions are solitary hunters that depend on stalking and ambush tactics to take down prey often seven times their size!

Just before dusk, Eric (a client) went to relieve himself in the toilet area 200 feet (61 m) from the tent site. As he was leaving the area, he noticed a slight movement in the woods in front of him. He instinctively froze and found himself looking at a mountain lion approximately 25 feet (7.6 m) in front of him. Eric immediately tried to make himself look bigger by raising his arms over his head and started yelling for help, startling the lion and causing it to run into the woods. Tim and Jan arrived along with a couple of others and told Eric he had done a good job scaring off the lion.

Just before dark the lion showed up again, this time around the tent site giving everyone the feeling that they were being stalked. This sighting unnerved the entire group. Tim and Jan started a campfire and decided that each group member would take a turn during the night on mountain lion watch.

Accidents, Incidents, and Misadventures

1. Is lighting a campfire and setting up a watch the best approach to deal with this situation? Why or why not?

2. Given the available resources, was there a better way for the guides to address this potentially dangerous situation? Explain your answer.

3. Mountain lion attacks are on the increase. What are the do's and don'ts when it comes to mountain lion safety?

4. Investigate mountain lion attacks in the United States. What interesting facts did you find?

Black Bear Problem

The Wilderness Base Camp Adventure Program is located on 90 acres of leased land managed by the U.S. Forest Service. The base camp has a dining hall and kitchen facility, staff housing, an equipment warehouse, a food-packing building, student cabins, a bathhouse, and six satellite campsites each with a tent or tarp platform and cook area. The program operates year-round, with the majority of programs conducted from May through August. Recently, black bears have been coming into the base camp in search of food. Black bears are dangerous, curious, and adaptable. They quickly become accustomed to human activity, which can eventually lead to aggressive food-gathering habits.

Instructors have reported food bags being pilfered and carried away from the satellite campsites around the base camp, and on one occasion a student was bluff-charged after surprising a bear on the trail. The bears have also attempted to break into the food-packing building and early one morning broke through the screen door of the kitchen, ransacking it.

Bears have also been reported in the program's activity areas. On one occasion a bear walked into a campsite and left with the group's food bag, after the students had neglected to hang their food as required.

Program managers are becoming concerned that sooner or later the bears will become more aggressive and injure a student or staff member. They all agree that something has to be done.

QUESTIONS

1. Investigate black bear behavior. What are the dangers of interactions between humans and black bears?

2. What are some realistic deterrents that the program can take to mitigate the black bear problem?

3. What are some practices that the program should implement while the deterrents are put in place?

4. Create a risk management plan with specific guidelines for black bear encounters at base camp and one for the backcountry.

Smile for the Camera

During an adaptive Outward Bound program, students (13 to 15 years old) were on a final expedition in the Pocono Mountains of Pennsylvania; their instructors were following close behind. After a long and tiring morning, the group decided to take a lunch stop. After lunch they took a short nap. As the students slept, a black bear entered their "sleeping quarters" and tore through a backpack to access a bag of gorp. Hearing the commotion, a couple of students woke up and began taking pictures of the bear from approximately 10 feet (3 m) away. The bear left after posing for pictures and finishing off the gorp.

QUESTIONS

1. How would you have reacted in this situation if you were the instructors?
2. What are some proactive measures program administrators can take to address this potentially dangerous situation?
3. Was this near miss avoidable? Explain your answer.

Snakebite

The timber rattlesnake (*Crotalus horridus*) is one of four species of poisonous snakes found in North Carolina. These are heavy-bodied snakes that vary in color. The venom of timber rattlers is very toxic, and deaths from their bites have been recorded (Snakes of North Carolina, 2011).

Rick was an instructor at the Table Mountain Wilderness Program (TMWP) and a professional environmental educator with a genuine interest in reptiles, especially snakes. TMWP is located in Western North Carolina and offers multiday rock climbing, whitewater canoeing, backpacking, and challenge course experiences. The program embraces the principles of Leave No Trace and includes local and natural history in all of its programs.

Because the TMWP area is prime habitat for both poisonous and nonpoisonous snakes, the program director (a snake enthusiast) felt strongly that educating students on how to distinguish between poisonous and nonpoisonous snakes was important. The Snake Talk program was created for this purpose.

As part of the Snake Talk, TMWP kept a locked, partitioned cage (Plexiglas lid, plywood sides) that contained poisonous snakes (copperheads, timber rattlesnakes, and diamondback rattlesnakes) and nonpoisonous snakes (black rat snakes and garter snakes).

Before being allowed to handle the snakes, interested staff (no students) had to be checked out by the program director. Rick had considerable experience as a snake handler and had no problem passing the test. One afternoon a group of Rick's students gathered around the snake cage while Rick removed one of the timber rattlesnakes to discuss its physical characteristics.

Rick's presentation went well, as expected—after all, he was a snake expert and excellent teacher. At the completion of his program, Rick was putting the snake back into the cage when a student unexpectedly asked him a question. Caught off guard, Rick temporarily lost control of the snake, which immediately bit the base of his thumb on his right hand. Rick immediately placed the snake in the cage, locked it, and began to perform his own first aid. An assistant instructor herded the students away from the accident scene, while another staff member ran off to let the program director know what had happened.

A few minutes later, Rick was prepared for transport, placed in the back of a pickup truck, and driven to the nearest hospital over an hour away. By the time Rick arrived at the emergency room, he was in critical condition. It took every ounce of antivenin to save him. He was stabilized and transported by ambulance to a larger hospital with more resources

It is important to think about the impact of humans on wildlife *and* the effect wildlife can have on humans when thinking about risk management. Is it OK to handle wildlife when participating in outdoor or adventure programs? How can leaders prepare participants for the wildlife they might encounter?

Provided courtesy of Daniel W. Sanner.

and antivenin. Rick survived the ordeal and still works with snakes in the Florida Everglades.

QUESTIONS

1. Is there anything wrong with maintaining a cage full of snakes for educational purposes? Why or why not?

2. Is there a better way to teach students how to identify snakes?

3. What are the potential risk management issues with this scenario?

4. What is proper first aid for snakebite?

5. What recommendations do you have for TMWP to prevent this or a similar incident from happening again?

Proceed With Caution When River Crossing

River and stream crossings can be very dangerous and difficult at times. Everyone in the group should be able to cross at the chosen crossing point. If not, then the leader should seek another crossing option, even if it means altering the route or looking somewhere else. Several factors go into choosing the right place to cross, including water depth, the strength of the current, and runout (what the stream channel and stream bank look like downstream from the crossing point)—are there hazards or potential problems if someone falls into the river?

In one instance, five hikers on a personal backpacking trip in Colorado's Maroon Bell Wilderness attempted an early spring stream crossing using a rope for safety. The group tied a rope to trees on either stream bank to use as a handline to support them as they crossed the swollen stream. Glenn Martin (25), the last to cross, untied the rope from the tree and tied it to himself. He then held on to the rope and began to pull himself hand over hand across the stream. Midway through the crossing, he lost his footing and let go of the rope. He was immediately swept downstream in the swift current. Once he reached the end of the rope, he became submerged and was held underwater by the strong current. Eventually, one of the hikers was able to reach him and cut him free. With help from the others, he was able to pull Martin back to the stream bank, where they started CPR. After approximately 30 minutes they stopped resuscitation efforts. Martin was dead.

QUESTIONS

1. What are the rules regarding the use of a rope in a river or stream crossing?

2. What is the difference between a handline and a fixed line? Which is appropriate for river and stream crossings?

3. What are the do's and don'ts when it comes to river and stream crossings?

Student Drowns in a Stream Crossing

Jim Strong, an experienced outdoor guide, was contracted by a youth minister to help lead a group of eight 14- and 15-year-olds on a weekend backpacking trip. The purpose of the program was to get the students outdoors, introduce them to the demands of backcountry travel, and work on teambuilding skills. Prior to departure, Jim checked the weather report, which indicated intermittent showers throughout the weekend.

The group of eight students, Jim, and the youth minister left the church parking lot around 5:00 p.m. Friday evening and arrived at the campsite around 8:00 p.m. It rained on and off during the drive to the trailhead. The next morning the group woke up to a cloudy sky.

Following breakfast, the group followed the Flatbush Creek Trail out of camp. Approximately 3 miles (4.8 km) into the hike, the trail crossed Flatbush Creek. At this point, Jim stopped the group to assess the creek crossing. The creek had become rain-swollen overnight, which concerned Jim and he warned the youth minister about the dangers of crossing a rain-swollen stream. He later told investigators that Flatbush Creek at the point where the trail crosses is normally a simple stream crossing. He also reported that he told some of the students (not all were paying attention) to loosen the shoulder straps and hip belts on their backpacks so that if they fell into the water, they could remove their backpacks.

The youth minister appreciated Jim's concern and insisted that the group cross the creek at this point. It wasn't worth hiking the extra 2 miles (3.2 km) cross-country to cross the creek. A few minutes later Marsha (a student) tried to throw her sleeping bag across the stream (she was afraid it would get wet in the crossing). It didn't make it across; instead, the bag fell short and landed in the stream. The fast moving current began to carry it downstream. Marsha instinctively jumped into the stream to chase down her bag. She took a couple of steps, stumbled, and fell into the creek still wearing her backpack. She immediately went underwater and disappeared. Her lifeless body was recovered by her group approximately 200 feet (60 m) downstream from where she entered the water.

QUESTIONS

1. How is this scenario similar to the preceding one (Proceed With Caution When River Crossing)?

2. Investigate acceptable river and stream crossing practices. Which can you incorporate into your program? Discuss and demonstrate each of these techniques to your group.

3. Draw a section of a river or stream you are familiar with. Identify the direction of flow and various hydrological features of this section, along with prominent landscape features along the river or stream banks. Identify a safe place to cross. Why did you choose this site?

Drowning in a Forest Pool

Swimming in the backcountry can create a number of risk management concerns for outdoor leaders. Deep, cold moving or shallow water, water with poor visibility, uneven bottoms, slippery rocks, steep terrain, and a lack of rescue equipment are some of the problems backcountry aquatic environments can create. Instructors and guides should evaluate whether a site is safe for swimming, assess the comfort and skill level of participants, and know how to improvise rescue equipment with available resources.

Deshaun Winaver (17) and seven other students from an inner-city alternative public school left town on Tuesday morning. That night they slept in a nearby national forest campground 20 miles (32 km) from a paved highway.

The next day, as other students watched, Deshaun jumped into a deep pool in the middle of a fast current, went under, and drowned. Reports indicate that Deshaun entered the water on his own accord. Other students were in the immediate area, and teachers were nearby. It was noted that the strong undercurrents from the waterfall were a contributing factor. After receiving an emergency call from a teacher with a cell phone, rescue workers got to the scene in two hours.

QUESTIONS

1. In your opinion, could this tragedy have been prevented?

2. What techniques, approaches, or practices could or should have been implemented to prevent this tragic accident?

3. Investigate programs that teach leaders how to screen participants' swimming ability, evaluate backcountry aquatic sites, and improvise rescue techniques. Share your findings with your group.

Student Drowns After Jumping Into Backcountry Swimming Hole

Brady Williams (16) panicked and drowned after leaping into California's McCloud River. Williams was one of a dozen teenage boys attending a weeklong outdoor activity trip in July 2010. The boys were based at the Outdoor Education Center and had been rock climbing and rappelling earlier in the day. They hiked to the river late in the afternoon to cool off. The boys were instructed to keep their boots on to protect their feet and began jumping into the pool 25 feet (7.6 m) below.

Witnesses described the efforts made to save Williams after he jumped in and immediately began to panic. Witnesses also said that Jade Turner, one of the instructors, encouraged Williams to jump. Some of the boys noted that Turner said he would save Williams if he jumped and that Williams replied that if Turner didn't, he would drown. Turner dismissed the boys' statement and insisted that the conversation had never happened. He said he had never spoken with Williams and had not encouraged him to jump. He added that he had called on the other instructor to join him in the pool, but the instructor had declined. When Williams jumped, Turner was the only person in the water and immediately went to his aid. Turner described how he had been unable to save Williams as he struggled and was forced to let go and leave the pool to remove his boots before returning.

"Brady started to panic, flapping his arms and pushing down on my head to keep himself afloat," said Turner. "This happened three or four times. I kept getting pushed under. I was finding it hard to breathe. I was swallowing a lot of water, and I realized I was getting into trouble myself."

Turner reported that the other instructor eventually came into the pool to relieve him and was soon followed by one of the older students. The older student told authorities that Williams told him hours before that he could not swim but intended to jump into the swimming hole anyway. He immediately warned him against doing so and told him he would drown if he did. Turner said he remembered Williams telling the older student that he could not swim when the students were asked about their abilities before going to the pool. He said Williams then claimed he could swim "a little," adding that he believed the change of mind had been because he did not want to be excluded from the activity.

QUESTIONS

1. What are the differences among swimming, dipping, and wading? Which of these activities are permissible in your program?

2. Should adventure programs have a policy that addresses each of the activities in question 1?

3. What are the primary factors that contributed to this tragedy?

4. How could this accident have been prevented?

5. What is a water comfort test? What role could this assessment play in preventing drowning?

Rescue Teams Save Church Group

A youth group on a faith-building "survivor challenge" got into rough water, triggering a massive rescue effort on the Uwharrie River. Emergency workers rescued all 30 boaters—six adults and the rest children 10 to 12 years old with no injuries reported. The County Emergency Management Director said one of the adults used a cell phone to call 911 from a boat, saying the group had gotten separated in fast-moving water.

The children were participating in an event called the "Survivor Challenge," organized by God's Country Outfitters, which hosts outdoor adventure experiences for religious groups. The three-day event is described as an opportunity "to overcome your fears through physical challenges, build community through group activities, and grow in confidence to do God's work." The associate pastor of the church told reporters: "I'm sure that it was a great adventure for the children to see God's hand in their lives."

Around noon Thursday, the group launched kayaks and canoes into the Uwharrie River at Low Water Bridge, a narrow wooden structure near NC 109, about eight miles northwest of Troy and 50 miles east of Charlotte. The river is near Morrow Mountain State Park and flows through the Uwharrie National Forest. Low Water Bridge is a well-known access spot to the river for kayakers and canoeists.

The river can be unpredictable especially after a heavy rain. The water was so high Thursday that Low Water Bridge was submerged beneath quickly moving clay-colored water.

Morrow Mountain State Park rangers noted that the water level rose several inches soon after the group got into the water. Authorities were called at 12:16 p.m. and told that between 22 and 30 people were in need of rescue. Cell phone communication is spotty in that part of the county, and for a while, it appeared as if a large portion of the group was missing. There were also initial reports that boaters were stuck in trees, though this turned out to be false.

Swift-water rescue teams from three adjoining counties sped to the river to help. N.C. National Guard helicopters carrying crews that included firefighters from Charlotte, and N.C. Highway Patrol helicopters were also summoned, though those calls were ultimately canceled. Randolph County Emergency Management officials said seven people were rescued several hundred yards from Low Water Bridge. Others were picked up where the river dumped into Lake Tillery, about four miles downstream from the bridge.

Adapted, by permission, from C.R. Wootson, Jr. and S. Lyttle, 2009, "Rescue teams save church group," *The Charlotte Observer.*

1. What objective, subjective, and leadership factors contributed to this incident?

2. In your opinion, who was at fault, the outfitter or the church group? Explain your answer.

3. What guidelines should your program follow when choosing a guide or outfitter?

Open Canoes Over Open Water

During the early morning of April 12, 2010, a group of six students, a parent, a teacher, and an experienced paddling guide began a daylong open canoe paddle over open water to a small offshore island. Everyone was wearing PFDs. None of the boats were equipped with spray decks, flares, or radios. The weather report called for west winds of 1 to 5 knots (2 to 9 km/hr) with gusts up to 10 knots (19 km/hr) and increasing to around 20 to 30 knots (37 to 56 km/hr). Seas were expected to be 1 to 2 feet (30 to 60 cm) and increasing to 3 to 4 feet (90 to 120 cm). Their plan was to explore the island as part of a marine biology class, have lunch, and then paddle the 2 miles (3.2 km) back to the mainland. Their estimated time of arrival was 5:00 or 6:00 p.m.

The group arrived at the island, explored, had lunch, and began the paddle back to the mainland. Approximately 30 minutes into the trip, the parent began to have some physical problems. The guide took notice and began to tend to the parent. She asked the teacher to raft the students together. Once the students had rafted up to the teacher's boat, they began to drift into open water eventually losing contact with the guide and the parent.

As predicted, the winds and wave height increased, causing each of the open canoes to swamp, forcing all six students and the teacher into the water. School officials became worried when the group hadn't returned by 7:00 p.m. and contacted the Coast Guard for assistance. The Coast Guard began an aerial search and immediately found the parent and guide. The rest of the group was picked up by helicopter an hour later. Unfortunately, three students drowned in this tragic incident.

QUESTIONS

1. What are the risk management issues inherent in this scenario?

2. What are some options the group could have exercised given the circumstances?

3. What pre-trip guidelines for best management practices would you outline for an incident like this?

4. This is a low-frequency, high-severity incident. What recommendation(s) would you make to the school's administration regarding the future of this program? Use the potential frequency and severity of loss model to assist you in your decision.

5. This was "only" a marine biology trip. Should this type of activity follow the same policies and procedures that more traditional adventure or guided programs follow? Explain your answer.

Equipment

Technology can play a significant role in the success or failure of outdoor adventure and guided programs and activities. Various forms of technology have become more visible in the outdoor adventure industry primarily through access and innovations in transportation, comfort, safety, communication, and information (Ewert & Schultis, 1999). Technological devices found in backcountry recreation range from relatively simple inflatable sleeping pads and camp stoves to complex handheld global positioning systems (GPS), personal locator beacons (PLBs), and avalanche transceivers and high-tech fabrics and materials. Cell and satellite phones have also become important resources for program staff, guides, and backcountry search and rescue teams.

TECHNOLOGY AND ADVENTURE AND GUIDED PROGRAMS

Because technology pervades our lives, many people expect certain devices to be available on backcountry outings. In anticipation of this, guide services and adventure program providers should disclose what will and will not be available to participants during the adventure experience. When certain expected equipment is not available, program directors have an obligation to disclose why (Hansen-Stamp & Gregg, 2002). However, cell or satellite phones do not belong in this category. The industry standard for commercial operations is to carry appropriate communication equipment.

All programs should develop criteria or policies regarding the use of cell or satellite phones and other electronic devices (e.g., personal locator beacons, personal satellite trackers). The *Policy for Field Communication Devices* (North Carolina Outward Bound, 2010) includes the following policy: Field communication devices will be used by staff in the conduct of Outward Bound business in emergency situations, or if staff have a situation that is beyond their ability to manage in the field. Appropriate examples of use include:

- Emergency notification or response
- Medical or behavioral management consultation
- Logistical or evacuation problem-solving that would reduce the need for extraordinary driving, etc.

Personal locator beacons (PLBs) are relatively new communication devices being used by the public and some outdoor programs and guides. PLBs are portable units that operate like the emergency position indicating radio beacon (EPIRBs) used by mariners or the emergency locator transmitters (ELTs) used by aviators. PLBs are carried by individuals and, unlike some EPIRBs and ELTs, can be activated only manually. PLBs can be detected anywhere in the world by global satellites. They contain a built-in, low-power beacon that transmits on 121.5 megahertz allowing rescuers to hone in on the distress signal with signal locator technology.

NONTECHNICAL AND TECHNICAL EQUIPMENT

Adventure programs and guide services use both technical and nontechnical equipment to conduct their programs (Blanchard, Strong, & Ford, 2007). Nontechnical equipment includes items such as camp cookware, hats, gloves, boots, maps, and compasses. The condition of nontechnical items may affect user comfort but should not have major safety implications. The equipment and clothing requirements for an outdoor program usually depend on the geographic location, the activity itself, the length of the activity, the type of terrain and environment, the time of year, and the weather.

Technical equipment is used in activities that require specialized training (Blanchard, Strong, & Ford, 2007). Such equipment may need regular maintenance above and beyond the checks carried out prior to or after each use. Some equipment (e.g., backpacks) may need to be adjusted by a qualified person before each use; other equipment (e.g., climbing ropes) requires careful record keeping each time it is used. For example, rope use is documented through the use of a rope log that keeps track of the date of use, what the rope was used for, and any damage. This procedure, along with proper use and care of the ropes, will help ensure that the rope and associated equipment are properly maintained. Failure to use or inappropriate use of technical equipment is likely to have a direct impact on the safety of the user. Also, the management of technical equipment requires a higher level of skill, knowledge, and experience than does the management of nontechnical equipment. Technical equipment includes climbing harnesses, stoves, canoes, kayaks, skis, communication devices (e.g., cell and satellite phones), and navigational equipment (e.g., personal locator beacons, GPS units, satellite trackers, and other similar devices).

Adventure programs and guide services implement systems to ensure that only the staff members leading the activity have access to technical equipment, and that those staff members have the qualifications to use it.

How does technical equipment differ from nontechnical equipment? What technical and nontechnical equipment would you need to go on a three-day hike that will include kayaking?

iofoto/fotolia.com

All adventure program providers should ensure that technical equipment is used correctly and that participants receive activity-specific training.

PERSONAL PROTECTION EQUIPMENT

Program providers also have a duty to maintain, clean, and replace personal protection equipment (PPE). Commonly used PPE include ropes, carabiners, helmets, harnesses, and personal flotation devices. In almost all program settings, PPE is provided free of charge to employees; some programs charge a small rental fee to participants.

Programs that allow participants to provide their own PPE should check each item before it is used. PPE is appropriate only if it is suitable for the risks and the conditions for which it was designed, takes into consideration both employee and participant needs, meets government regulations and industry standards, and most important, fits properly and provides protection.

In addition to inspecting PPE before each use, in-depth inspections should be carried out by competent and experienced inspectors. The frequency of the in-depth inspection should be governed by the type and intensity of use. Manufacturers have implemented guidelines to take the guesswork out of when, what, and how to inspect specific articles of technical equipment (Petzl, 2010).

EQUIPMENT LOGISTICS

Good equipment management also includes providing secure storage space, ventilation, and a system for booking equipment use and logging equipment in and out. Schedules should be established for the preventive maintenance of equipment. Following are some additional equipment management considerations:

- Equipment should be used only for activities for which it was manufactured.
- All equipment should be individually identified and coded. Purchase dates should be noted on each piece of equipment.
- The life span of all pieces of equipment should be recorded, so they can be disposed of at the appropriate time.
- If there is any question about the condition of a piece of equipment, it should be withdrawn from use.
- Regular routine checks should be made on all equipment. This information should be documented.
- Equipment should be stored correctly.
- When in doubt about any piece of equipment, staff members should seek the advice of a technical expert.

Before issuing any technical equipment, instructors or guides should inspect it themselves or ask participants to check for any damage. When equipment is returned, qualified staff members should check for wear or damage, clean it as appropriate, dry it out, make any small repairs, and store it so it is ready for use (Blanchard, Strong, & Ford, 2007). The best plan for managing technical equipment is to put only one person or a small number of people in charge of it. A program equipment manager (or managers) should be responsible for logging, checking, maintaining and repairing, and replacing equipment.

A log book or other record-keeping method should be used to record purchase dates and days of use, and to make certain that technical equipment is inspected on a regular basis, that proper maintenance is done, and that the equipment is retired or disposed of at the end of its life span. To maintain product traceability, markings or labels should not be removed from any article of equipment. Instructors and guides should be in the habit of checking equipment before it is used to ensure that it is in operating condition and suitable for its intended use. If equipment is checked out of a central location, adequate systems should be in place for logging each item in and out.

CLOTHING

Clothing is an important risk management consideration. Instructors and guides should be able to explain why a particular article of clothing or equipment is required. This information will be helpful to participants who have concerns about spending money on unnecessary clothing or are worried about the amount of weight they will be carrying on their backs. Clothing required in an adventure program setting should be selected based on its ability to protect participants from the elements (rain, snow, and wind) and to keep them comfortable during a variety of activities and weather conditions.

To ensure that participants arrive with the required clothing for their particular outings or programs, instructors and guides should distribute clothing lists well before the event. Clothing lists should vary based on the activity and the season.

SUMMARY

The use of technology has become more noticeable in the outdoor adventure industry primarily through access and transportation, comfort, safety, communication, and information. Because technology is part of our daily lives, outdoor program participants expect that technology, especially communication devices, will be available during backcountry trips.

Both technical and nontechnical equipment is used by adventure program providers. Nontechnical equipment may affect the comfort of the user but should not have major safety implications. Technical equipment, on the other hand, is used in activities that require specialized training and is usually safety related. Equipment and clothing requirements are dependent on the geographic location of the program, the activity itself, the length of the activity, the type of terrain and environment, the time of year, and the weather.

All equipment requires regular maintenance and careful record keeping. Programs should develop systems to ensure that the staff members leading activities have the necessary qualifications, that technical equipment is used correctly, and that participants are appropriately trained in its use. Good equipment management also requires secure storage space, ventilation, and a system for logging equipment in and out. Schedules should be established for the preventive maintenance of equipment.

Stranded Hiker Uses Personal Locator Beacon to Summon Help

On the evening of December 30th, the U.S. Air Force notified Big Bend National Park that a personal locator beacon (PLB) signal had been received from a backcountry location within the park. Rangers headed to a backcountry campsite about six miles from the coordinates given by the PLB and found a vehicle registered to a visitor who had a solo hiker permit for that zone of the park. Two rangers then hiked to the approximate PLB coordinates, but were unable to find anyone in that area.

Another team of searchers and a Texas Department of Public Safety (DPS) helicopter joined them the following morning. The crew of the helicopter homed in on the 121.5 MHz distress transmissions from the PLB within minutes of arriving on scene and soon spotted the hiker, who was waving a space blanket at them. He had "cliffed out" (the hiker reached an impasse and could not ascend or descend because of the steepness of the vertical terrain) on the side of Elephant Tusk Peak, but gave the helicopter crew a thumbs-up signal indicating that he was okay. Although the helicopter was unable to land, the crew directed searchers to the man's location, then ferried rope and climbing equipment to the rangers on scene. They climbed to his location and helped him down.

The man told rangers that he'd attempted to climb to the top of Elephant Tusk the day before. He'd cached his backpack, tent and sleeping bag and had made the ascent carrying only a space blanket, food, water, a whistle, an LED light, and a PLB. After topping a 40-foot (12 m) chimney, he decided to turn back—only to find he couldn't climb down from his location. He spent the night on a 6-foot by 50-foot (1.8 m by 15.2 m) ledge wrapped in the space blanket, with his PLB tied to a bush to keep it from being blown away by high winds. Overnight temperatures were just below freezing. This incident marks the first time in Big Bend that a PLB has been used by a hiker to call in rescuers. Without the PLB and assistance from the DPS helicopter, it would have been extremely difficult to find and rescue the man in a timely fashion. The PLB probably saved his life.

Adapted from M. Spier, 2007, "Stranded hiker uses personal locator beacon to summon help," *NPS Morning Report.*

QUESTIONS

1. How does a PLB work? Conduct an online search.
2. Should federal land managers require all backcountry visitors to carry PLBs? Explain your answer.

3. Do you believe outdoor program providers would take greater risks if they thought they could easily call in a rescue? Why or why not?
4. Would there be unintended consequences of requiring adventure programs to carry communication devices? Explain your answer.

Hikers Evacuated After Three SPOT Activations in Three Days

On the evening of September 23rd, Grand Canyon National Park rangers began a search for hikers who repeatedly activated their rented SPOT satellite tracking device (a type of PLB). The GEOS Emergency Response Center in Houston reported that someone in the group of four hikers—two men and their two teenage sons—had pressed the "help" button on their SPOT unit. The coordinates for the signal placed the group in a remote section of the park, most likely on the challenging Royal Arch loop. Due to darkness and the remoteness of the location, rangers were unable to reach them via helicopter until the following morning. When found, they'd moved about a mile and a half to a water source. They declined rescue, as they'd activated the device due to their lack of water. Later that same evening, the same SPOT device was again activated, this time using the "911" button. Coordinates placed them less than a quarter mile from the spot where searchers had found them that morning. Once again, nightfall prevented a response by park helicopter, so an Arizona DPS helicopter whose crew utilized night vision goggles was brought in. They found that the members of the group were concerned about possible dehydration because the water they'd found tasted salty, but no actual emergency existed. The helicopter crew declined their request for a night evacuation, but provided them with water before departing.

On the following morning, another SPOT "help" activation came in from the group. This time they were flown out by park helicopter. All four refused medical assessment or treatment. The group's leader had reportedly hiked once at the Grand Canyon; the other adult had no Grand Canyon and very little backpacking experience. When asked what they would have done without the SPOT device, the leader stated, "We would have never attempted this hike." The group leader was issued a citation for creating a hazardous condition (36 CFR 2.34(a)(4)).

Adapted from B. Torres, 2009, "Hikers evacuated after three SPOT activations in three days," *NPS Morning Report.*

QUESTIONS

1. What are the pros and cons of PLBs? Make a recommendation to your program director to use them or not use them in your program.

2. Create a policy for your program for the use of PLBs.

3. How does the use of a PLB in this scenario differ from that in the previous scenario (Stranded Hiker Uses Personal Locator Beacon to Summon Help)? Why is the use of a PLB acceptable in the previous scenario, but not in this one?

4. How would you introduce participants to PLBs and educate them about their appropriate use?

5. Investigate the SPOT Satellite GPS Messenger. Is this a better choice than a PLB for outdoor adventure programs? Explain your answer.

6. Should PLBs be standard gear for groups? Explain your answer.

7. What responsibilities should rest with the owner of the PLB?

Anchor Fails, Student Sues

Advances in climbing wall technology have made significant strides since the first commercial climbing gym opened in the United States in 1987. Today, gyms of varying sizes, designs, materials, and equipment are found in a variety of settings, attracting climbers of all abilities.

Steve Smith and his partner, Shamika Green, were participating in an indoor climbing class, a popular physical education activity at their high school. A climbing wall built over 15 years ago was the centerpiece of the climbing program. Both students elected to begin their session by warming up on a relatively easy climb. Smith, belayed by Green, was able to complete the 25-foot (7.6 m) climb without difficulty. After reaching the top, he yelled "Take!" and asked Green to lower him. Approximately 15 feet (4.6 m) from the ground, the 1-inch (2.5 cm) tubular webbing top rope anchor secured to the roof rafter tore sending Smith to the ground. Smith sustained serious injuries to his back.

According to the accident report, a student who had climbed the route earlier in the week had told physical education teacher, Ginito Suarez, that the webbing looked frayed. Anderson's response to the student was that he would inspect and replace the anchor sling. Smith's family is suing the high school for his injuries.

QUESTIONS

1. What is periodic maintenance? What does it include? How often should it be performed?

2. Research climbing anchors for indoor climbing walls. Can you recommend a better top rope anchor system for this climbing facility?

3. What are the responsibilities of instructional staff? Is maintenance one of those responsibilities? Explain your answer.

4. Was the high school negligent given the facts presented? Explain your answer.

5. What role does a climbing wall inspection play in reducing risk?

6. Create a climbing wall inspection checklist for your facility.

7. How often should indoor climbing wall ropes be replaced? What about helmets, harnesses, and other rock climbing equipment?

8. Should helmets be required in indoor climbing gyms? Why or why not?

9. What are the industry practices for operating an indoor climbing gym?

10. Why is documentation a critical element of risk management?

Fall From Climbing Wall

Automatic belay systems are becoming increasingly popular in indoor climbing gyms as the interest in climbing grows. This was the case in a local climbing gym. During a supervised summer school climbing program, Aidan, a 12-year-old boy, along with five other students ages 12 to 14 and three chaperones, was driven to the Rock World Climbing Gym to spend the morning climbing. The three chaperones were charged with the duty of supervising and monitoring the behavior of the six students. None of the chaperones were trained, nor were they knowledgeable about or experienced in any aspect of technical rock climbing.

The owner of Rock World, Mr. Calhoun, fitted them with climbing shoes, helped them put on and adjust their harnesses, and showed them how to clip the climbing rope into their harnesses. Following these initial tasks, Mr. Calhoun asked one of the students to help him demonstrate the automatic belay system they were going to use during their visit.

What are some of the risks associated with using rock climbing walls? What can organizations do to prevent them?

Joanna Zielinska/fotolia.com

The automatic belay is a mechanical system used to arrest a falling climber without the assistance of a human belayer. The system also lowers the climber gently to the ground once the climber reaches the top of the climbing route. The demonstration required that the student climb an easy route to the top of the wall, and upon reaching the top, lean back and have the automatic belay system safely lower him to the floor

Following the demonstration, Mr. Calhoun asked if there were any questions. The students and chaperones had no questions. At that point, Mr. Calhoun told the students that they could "climb anywhere in the gym." Thereafter,

Aidan and the other students began climbing routes on the various walls in the gym while the three chaperones watched and supervised their behavior. Aidan, excited about climbing, completed three climbs. Each time he climbed, he was watched by one of the chaperones as the automatic belay system lowered him safely to the floor.

Later in the morning, Aidan, William (a student), and a chaperone entered another area of the gym. Aidan immediately walked over to one of the ropes, clipped in, and began to climb. He completed the 25-foot (7.6 m) climb and leaned back anticipating that the automatic belay system would lower him to the floor as before. Instead, he became airborne falling the entire 25 feet (7.6 m) to the floor, landing on his feet and then falling backward before coming to rest on his back on the padded surface. Unknown to the chaperone and to Aidan, he had clipped into a rope that was not attached to an automatic belay system; that climb was set up as a manual belay! He suffered serious leg and back injuries.

QUESTIONS

1. What are the advantages and disadvantages of the automatic belay system?

2. Investigate the history of the automatic belay system. Share your findings with your group.

3. Is it industry standard to use automatic belay systems? Why or why not?

4. How much responsibility for this incident rests with the chaperones? How much rests with the gym owner, Mr. Calhoun? How much rests with Aidan? Explain your answer.

5. In hindsight, what could have been done to prevent this accident?

6. Was negligence involved in this accident? If you answered yes, identify each component.

7. Create a lesson plan for a day of climbing. Use the situation and resources described in this scenario.

8. Create a lesson plan for teaching the automatic belay system and auto locking or auto assist belay devices (e.g., Grigri, Cinch, and others). Compare and contrast these devices to tube or plate-type belay devices.

Instructor's Inattention Blamed for Student's Death

Zip lines, once found exclusively in adventure programs, are becoming more mainstream; they have become popular at outdoor adventure camps and resorts, and as commercial ventures. Travis Hopkins (40) was a participant in a zip line adventure at Zips USA. According to reports, he fell 30 feet (9 m) to his death from a zip line after an employee failed to attach Travis correctly to the zip line. Witnesses said the employee, Mack (a recently unemployed delivery truck driver), was described as having a complacent attitude toward safety. This became clear when a witness described a previous incident involving another person in the group who had fallen off the zip line. He was spared injury (or worse) when he was caught by a backup system.

Evidently, Mack did not stop the activity long enough to assess the potential cause of the problem. In addition, Mack did not conduct any additional checks to test the integrity of the equipment to make sure it was suitable for use. Instead, he continued to send participants down the zip line as if nothing had happened.

When confronted by investigators, the program provider insisted that safety inspections and employee evaluations were conducted before Travis' fatal accident. When asked by investigators for the reports, the owner stated that Zips USA doesn't document this information because the paperwork creates legal problems.

QUESTIONS

1. In your opinion, what should the minimum training requirements be for an instructor or guide operating a zip line?

2. What topics should be included in a staff training session for this activity?

3. What are some ways instructors can make sure safety systems are in place prior to conducting activities?

4. What do you think of the fact that Zips USA does not document inspections because the paperwork creates legal problems? Why is documentation an important risk management control?

5. Investigate other zip line incidents by conducting an Internet search. Describe each incident and identify its cause as best you can. Did your investigation identify any patterns or trends?

6. Based on your findings from question 5, can you make some recommendations for reducing zip line incidents?

Repair Kits Can Be Deadly

The Southwest Outdoor Education Program (SOEP) is a high adventure program for teenagers designed to build self-confidence and teach social and problem-solving skills. One of the program's primary activities is a multiday rafting experience on Utah's Green River. The Green is a relatively calm river with class I and II rapids and an occasional class III found along its 84-mile (135 km) length. This, combined with the river's remote backcountry setting, beautiful scenery, sand beaches, and red rock canyons, makes the Green an ideal venue for SOEP programs.

While loading rafts one morning, an SOEP instructor noticed that a thwart in one of the rafts had deflated overnight. Upon further inspection, she noted a small tear in the fabric. Seeing this as a teachable moment, she asked the students to stop what they were doing and observe her as she patched the damaged thwart.

She opened the raft repair kit and shared its contents with her students. One of the items in the kit was Barge Cement, an all-purpose contact glue that is water resistant and ideal for raft repair. The students watched as the instructor attached the patch to the damaged thwart.

Once the thwart was repaired and inflated, the group continued to break camp and load the rafts for another long day on the river.

Following dinner that evening, the group sat down around a campfire to reflect on the day's events. Everyone was present except David, one of the students. After calling his name, instructors became concerned when he didn't answer. The three instructors decided to do a hasty search around the campsite. One instructor was to walk down to the river, another was to check the spring behind the camp, and the other was to check the latrine area. Moments later, the instructor conducting the search by the river yelled, "I found him!" David was lying unconscious in one of the rafts; the repair kit was open and an open tube of Barge Cement and a plastic bag lay by his side.

The instructor's initial assessment revealed shallow respirations and a weak pulse. Instructors used their satellite phone to call for an evacuation. Instructors monitored him while waiting for medical transport. A Life Flight helicopter arrived approximately one hour later. David was transported to a regional hospital where he died from what doctors described as inhalant abuse.

QUESTIONS

1. Research to discover what the active ingredient is in Barge Cement that makes it ideal for abuse. Investigate this ingredient further by

referencing a material safety data sheet (MSDS). What are the dangers associated with this substance?

2. Are there any other substances commonly carried on a backcountry trip that could be abused by participants?

3. Once you have identified these substances, create a protocol for your program to address the potential abuse of these substances.

Automated External Defibrillator in the Woods

An automated external defibrillator (AED) is a medical device that automatically analyzes heart rhythm. If it detects a problem, it responds with an electrical shock to disrupt or stop the heart's dysrhythmic electrical activity. Because of their relatively small size and ease of use, AEDs have been installed in schools, airports, and other public places. According to the American Heart Association, electric defibrillation and AEDs improve the survival rates of CPR rescue attempts by as much as 49 percent.

After successfully purchasing and installing a number of AEDs throughout a university recreation complex, Irisbel, the campus recreation director, thought that it would be a good idea for outdoor adventure program leaders to carry AEDs on all of their land- and water-based outings. Irisbel is a strong proponent of risk management and believes that an AED will create a feeling of safety among participants. The adventure program includes many land- and water-based events during weekends and longer trips during fall, winter, and summer breaks. Ron, the adventure program director, is adamantly against the idea, arguing that AEDs weigh around 6 pounds (2.7 kg) and cost approximately $500 (USD) per unit.

Irisbel has asked Ron for a response outlining the program's position on this highly controversial request.

QUESTIONS

1. What are your views on the use of AEDs in backcountry settings?

2. What is the practicality of carrying and using an AED in a backcountry setting?

3. How would you respond to Irisbel's request? Why would an AED not be a practical medical or safety device to carry in a field setting? Why would it be?

4. What is the current industry standard for AEDs in the backcountry?

5. In what adventure program settings would the use of an AED be appropriate?

Stove Fueling Incident Causes Serious Burns

New materials and designs have resulted in backpacking stoves that are portable and lightweight. They are great for use in remote locations. Some stoves are engineered to burn multiple fuels. When used properly, they are safe and efficient. However, when used inappropriately, they become a significant backcountry hazard with the potential to cause serious injury.

A group of eight students and their two instructors were camping at a commercial campground after completing a 10-day backpacking expedition in Colorado's San Juan Mountains. The group was planning to resupply and then be transported to Indian Peaks Wilderness to complete their program.

Upon reaching the campground, the students set up camp and began to cook dinner using alcohol-fueled stoves. Both Ruth and Mike (assistant instructors) observed students go through the stove assembly and lighting. Mike continued to check in with the group while they were cooking. Ruth was on the satellite phone checking in with base camp. The students had set up their cook site surrounded by their tents.

Students April, Mark, and Chris were all sitting in a circle approximately 2 feet (61 cm) from their two stoves when Mark noticed that one of their stoves had gone out. He felt the stove burner and thought that it felt cool and that the flame was out (this check took approximately 2 seconds). He handed the stove to Chris, who began to pour fuel into the burner. In the process, the fuel stream burst into flames and ignited the remainder of the fuel in the bottle.

The bottle shot out of Chris' hand. The lit contents of the bottle shot over April, who was positioned across from Chris, lying on her side facing the stove with her hand supporting her head. The flame hit April in the torso and her clothes caught fire. April rolled on the ground several times, but was unable to extinguish the flames. April got up and started running. At this point Mike smothered the flames with a tarp. The entire incident was over in less than a minute.

The instructors called EMS via their satellite phone. When EMS arrived 30 minutes later, April was assessed, IV fluids were administered, and she was sedated for transport. Ruth accompanied April to the hospital. At the hospital, April was put into the intensive care unit and given anesthesia. Her burns were cleaned, pieces of clothing were removed, and her parents were contacted.

QUESTIONS

1. Identify all of the things that were done wrong in this scenario.

2. What changes would you make to prevent this situation from occurring?

3. What is the difference between general and specific supervision? What role should specific supervision have played in this scenario?

Boiling Water Fills Boot

Instructors rushing to get out of camp early one morning instructed students to set a pot of water on the top of two stoves set side by side to get water boiling for breakfast. Anna, one of the students, was stirring the pot of water as it was nearing a boil when it fell off the stoves, spilling boiling water into her boot and causing a partial thickness burn. She immediately removed her boot and immersed her foot in a nearby stream for approximately 15 minutes. This action relived the pain. Instructors covered her foot with a sterile dressing. Because of the location of the second-degree burn and the potential for infection, Anna had to leave the course.

QUESTIONS

1. What subjective, or human, factors contributed to this accident?

2. How would you set up a backcountry kitchen to prevent this and other stove-related injuries from occurring?

3. What is standard first aid for burns of this type in the backcountry?

Boiling Water Scalds

A group of canoeists in the North Woods of Maine was settling in for the evening on a small island located on Heap Big Lake. The campsite was managed by the local national forest and contained multiple tent sites, a pit toilet, and a picnic table constructed out of recycled plastic. Some students were setting up tents while others began preparing the evening meal on the picnic table. Both instructors were setting up their tarp and getting ready for a relaxing evening.

Roger (a student) was lying on the picnic table bench near the stove sitting on the picnic table where a pot that contained boiling water, olive oil, and pasta was being heated. Another student was monitoring the pot. Without warning, the pot fell off the stove spilling its contents onto the picnic table and splashing some onto Roger's back, soaking his clothing from his shoulder to his waist and upper thigh. Roger ripped off his shirt, and one of the instructors doused him with three liters of water; then flushed the burned area with water from the lake.

The instructors notified base camp via satellite phone, and the program's powerboat was dispatched to evacuate Roger. Upon arrival at the local hospital, Roger was diagnosed with second-degree burns on his shoulder, hip, and back. He subsequently left the course.

QUESTIONS

1. What caused the pot to fall off the stove? Should the instructors have anticipated this?

2. What are the common circumstances that led to each of these stove-related incidents (this one and the ones in the previous two scenarios)?

3. Develop a set of guidelines for stove use.

4. What activities could you incorporate into a staff training to address stove safety?

Transportation

Ask any outdoor program administrator, instructor, or guide to identify the most dangerous activity in which they engage, and without hesitation that person will tell you it is traveling in a motor vehicle to or from an activity site. In fact, research findings by the St. Paul Companies and Outward Bound identified driving and transportation as the area of greatest concern; it ranked above program activity, participant behavior, and environmental hazards (Moran et al., 2001). A primary reason transportation is of great concern to adventure and guided program providers is that managing the risks of the road is more difficult than managing the risks inherent in backcountry activities.

FIFTEEN-PASSENGER VANS

Adventure programs use a variety of vehicles to move participants and equipment to and from activity locations. Vans, buses, SUVs, watercraft, fixed and rotary winged aircraft, snowmobiles, dog sleds, horses, and other beasts of burden are some of the more common means of transportation. However, for the majority of programs, the 15-passenger van has been the primary vehicle of choice for transporting participants and equipment. Recently, the safety of the 15- passenger van has come under fire because of the documented rollover risks associated with these vehicles (National Highway Traffic Safety Administration, 2008). Rollover accidents occur when the driver loses control of the vehicle as a result of fatigue, overcompensation, or speeding. The number of documented rollover deaths associated with guided and adventure programs is unknown.

Vehicle Rollover

The potential for rollover exists when the combined weight of passengers raises the vehicle's center of gravity and causes it to shift rearward. As a result, the van has less resistance to rollover and handles differently making it more difficult to control in an emergency. Placing any load on the roof (once a common practice among adventure programs) also raises the center of gravity increasing the likelihood of a rollover.

The U.S. National Highway Traffic Safety Administration (NHTSA) (2008) data suggest that 95 percent of all single-vehicle rollovers are the result of tripping. Tripping occurs when a vehicle leaves the roadway and slides sideways, digging its tires into soft soil or striking a curb or guardrail; this applies a high tripping force to the tires and causes the vehicle to roll over. Rollover risk increases when 10 or more people are riding in a 15-passenger van, when the van is driven on rural roads, when the driver is driving too fast or is fatigued, or when the driver steers improperly or overcompensates (NHTSA, 2008). Ninety percent of rollovers occur after a driver has lost control of the vehicle and has run off the road (NHTSA, 2008).

Driver fatigue or speeding may cause a driver to lose control of a vehicle. Loss of control can cause the van to slide sideways off the road. Grass or earth medians can then cause the van to overturn when the tires contact the softer median surface. The driver can lose control when steering improperly or overcompensating as a panic reaction to an emergency, especially at freeway speeds. This can result in a sideways slide and consequent rollover.

Experienced Drivers

Because of its size, design, and handling characteristics, a 15-passenger van drives differently from other types of vehicles. One way guided and adventure programs address this issue is by limiting the number of drivers who will transport participants to activity sites. These drivers should receive ongoing professional training in the safe operation of vehicles, through in-house or national driver training programs such as the one developed by the U.S. National Safety Council (www.nsc.org/safety_road/Pages/safety_on_the_road.aspx). These programs can help drivers feel comfortable and have expertise and safety consciousness when handling vans.

Dual Rear Wheels

Retrofitting 15-passenger vans with dual rear wheels is not a new idea and has been considered by manufacturers for years. Research and testing suggest that adding dual rear wheels to each side of a 15-passenger van creates a more stable vehicle and improves its handling characteristics, thus reducing the risk of rollover. This retrofit also improves traction and load-carrying capability. It also decreases the likelihood of oversteering and the risk of rollover in emergency maneuvers.

Advocates for the retrofitting of dual rear wheels note that "Dual rear wheels will decrease the likelihood of dangerous oversteer characteristics and will decrease the risk of rollover in emergency maneuvers. Dual rear wheels are a technologically and economically feasible alternative because the manufacturers currently make large pick-up trucks with dual wheels comparable in size to these vans. Given the rising number of deaths and injuries associated with the vans, the economic cost for the manufacturers is minimal and the ethical obligation is clear" (Turner, 2002, p. 20).

TRANSPORTATION ALTERNATIVES

Some programs remove the back seat from oversized vehicles and limit the number of passengers to nine. The safety benefit of limiting passengers is lost, however, when the space created is used to carry equipment. In some instances programs have resorted to using 12-passenger vans, minivans, and SUVs along with support vehicles (e.g., pickup trucks) to carry equipment to reduce the dangers posed by 15-passenger vans. Minibuses are also being used. These vehicles resemble shortened school buses and are classified for 8 to 16 passengers. Secure cages are installed in the rear of some minibuses to carry equipment.

CONTROLLING TRANSPORTATION RISK

Administrative oversight can be an effective way to control transportation risks. Following are some common ways programs control transportation risks:

- Require driver background checks and documentation to ensure that potential drivers have clean driving records.
- Require drivers to have a certain number of years or miles of driving experience.
- Mandate a minimum age for drivers.
- Require that drivers pass both a written and road test for the vehicle and equipment (e.g., trailer).
- Limit the driving distance, hours of driving time, or number of passengers.
- Prohibit the use of personal vehicles for program-related trips or business.
- Post notices about safe driving, seat belt use, and other key topics in program vehicles.
- Implement an internal review process that designates who will be responsible for reviewing accidents, incidents, or failure to comply with driving policies.
- Identify and consistently apply consequences for accidents, incidents, or failure to comply with driving policies.

- Clearly define vehicle operating procedures that address all conditions and uses of the vehicle (e.g., cell phone and seat belt use).

Adventure program and guide services are beginning to use box and utility trailers to move equipment to and from activity sites as alternatives to rooftop cargo carriers. However, although towing a trailer has become a popular option, trailers create their own set of challenges. Once supervisors have determined that vehicles are appropriate for towing trailers, they need to answer additional questions (e.g., What is the towing capacity of the tow vehicle? Will the trailer need hydraulic or electric brakes? What is the height of the hitch point on the vehicle?).

Driving a vehicle with a trailer is very different from driving a trailerless vehicle or the family car. Because of this, the driver's driving style needs to change when towing a trailer. When towing, the driver has less room for error, the vehicle and trailer have limited maneuverability, and the driver must compensate for the length the trailer adds when changing lanes, turning, and cornering. Pulling a trailer also increases braking distances, fuel consumption, license and registration fees, and maintenance costs.

Programs need to be aware of the laws governing towing in their state or country. Finally, and most important, designated drivers should be properly trained.

MAINTENANCE

Regular maintenance is critical to ensure the safety, reliability, drivability, comfort, and longevity of program vehicles and trailers. Regular preventive care and maintenance of program vehicles can translate into economic benefits (e.g., fuel savings, increased resale values, less costly repairs later). Most important, periodic and preventive maintenance can help ensure the safety of participants. It can also prevent failures from occurring while the vehicle is being operated.

The driver is responsible for ensuring that the vehicle is in safe operating condition. To assist in this process, the outdoor program or guide service should have a procedure for vehicle inspection and a way to document the inspection. The driver is in an ideal position to notice problems and refer the vehicle to maintenance personnel for repairs. Program staff should be required to routinely check safety-related functions including, but not limited to, tires and spare tires, engine oil level, lights, mirrors, wipers, fluid levels, and belts. A pretrip checklist should be available for inspection and documentation purposes. A similar maintenance

Sometimes vehicle maintenance issues are the last things on a trip leader's mind. Organizations transporting participants do not have the luxury of forgetting to maintain their vehicles. What are some things that might need regular maintenance on a car, van, or bus?

Photo courtesy of Daniel W. Sanner.

and inspection checklist should also be used for trailers. Additional information on preventive maintenance and inspection procedures can be found on the U. S. Department of Transportation Federal Motor Carrier Safety Administration website (www.fmcsa.dot.gov/facts-research/research-technology/publications/accidenthm/vehicle.htm).

SUMMARY

Driving is one of the most dangerous activities undertaken by adventure programs; adventure program administrators consider it a major area of concern (Moran et al., 2001). Adventure programs use a variety of vehicles to transport participants and equipment to and from activity sites. The 15-passenger van has been the primary vehicle of choice by outdoor programs. Recently, the safety of the 15-passenger van has come under question as a result of research conducted by the U.S. National Highway Traffic Safety Administration (NHTSA). NHTSA found that passenger vans are prone to rollover when carrying more than 10 people. The weight of passengers raises the vehicle's center of gravity and causes it to shift rearward. This is compounded when equipment is carried on the vehicle's roof.

To address the danger of roof racks, many adventure programs and guide services use box and utility trailers to move equipment to and from activity sites. Some programs have retrofitted 15-passenger vans with dual rear wheels to improve traction and load-carrying capability. Removing the back seat in 15-passenger vans, using 12-passenger vans, using other types of vehicles, and administrative oversight are additional ways programs reduce the dangers posed by 15-passenger vans.

Regular vehicle maintenance is an important risk management consideration for adventure programs and guide services. In most programs, the driver is responsible for ensuring that the vehicle is in safe operating condition. The driver is also in a position to notice problems and refer the vehicle to maintenance personnel for repairs. To assist in this responsibility, programs should create procedures for vehicle inspections and documenting those inspections. Prior to any outing, program staff should be required to check safety-related functions using a pretrip checklist created by the organization. The following scenarios focus on the issues associated with managing transportation risk.

Narrow Road Proves to Be a Challenge

While providing support for a 23-day Rural Wilderness Program course, Keith (the driver) and Shirin, both logistics staff, were involved in a van accident while driving on a U.S. Forest Service road in Oregon's Willamette National Forest. Keith approached a particularly narrow, winding stretch of road when he came face to face with a logging truck driving in the middle of the road. Keith slowed down and began to move off the road to allow the larger vehicle to pass. The soft shoulder of the road gave way under the weight of the van. Keith attempted to move the vehicle back onto the road, but at that point the van rolled onto its side and headed down the steep embankment. Luckily, the van hit a tree, which caved in the roof, stopping the van. Keith and Shirin were able to exit the vehicle through the back door, which flew open during the rollover. Neither Keith nor Shirin was injured. The van was totaled.

QUESTIONS

1. Narrow, single-lane gravel roads are commonly used by outdoor programs to access trails, campsites, river put-ins and takeouts, and so on. Does your program's driver training include training on these types of roads?

2. What are some defensive driving tactics a van driver can use when driving on single-lane roads with blind corners?

3. What are some general defensive driving tactics a van driver can implement to reduce driving risks?

Road Conditions Create Problem for Van Driver

Twelve students and a driver from the Summit Backcountry School had just left the school's base camp in White Mountain National Forest en route to the airport when the driver took a blind curve wide, unintentionally allowing the vehicle's wheels to enter a deep rut remaining from the spring mud season. This caused the van to move closer to the edge of the road. The driver attempted to steer the vehicle out of the rut, but because of the slow speed of the vehicle and the depth of the rut, this was impossible. The vehicle eventually got to the edge of the road, where the shoulder collapsed, causing the van to roll over onto its side. Trees stopped the vehicle from continuing down the embankment. Everyone was able to exit the van via the undamaged driver-side door. Luckily, none of the seat-belted passengers were injured.

QUESTIONS

1. Is there a defensive driving technique that the driver could have implemented to avoid this accident?

2. How would your program respond to this scenario if there was a
   - High frequency of this type of incident with little or no injury?
   - Low frequency of this type of incident with serious injury?
   - Low frequency of this type of incident with little or no injury?
   - High frequency of this type of incident with serious injury?

   Answer this question by using the potential frequency and severity of loss model.

Tripping Incident

Tom, a whitewater specialist from the Fast Whitewater School, left the school's warehouse in a van loaded with rafts and rafting equipment. While driving down the narrow dirt road, Tom rounded a sharp curve and realized that he was much too close to the road edge on the right side. He stepped on the brake and attempted to turn back toward the center of the road. At this point the momentum of the vehicle was too great and the van continued to move forward; the right tire left the road. The van pitched to the right and rolled over, coming to rest with the driver's side down. Tom was wearing a seat belt and was not injured. He exited the van through the passenger door.

QUESTIONS

1. What are the common factors in each of the three van scenarios presented so far?

2. Conduct an e-mail survey to determine how outdoor adventure programs and guide services transport students and equipment given that roof racks are no longer appropriate for use.

3. Although none of the scenarios described so far involved rollovers, NHTSA has outlined a number of recommendations to reduce the risk of rollover injuries in 15-passenger vans. Review *Reducing the Risk of Rollover Crashes in 15 Passenger Vans* (riskmanagement.wsu. edu/utils/File.aspx?fileid=4221) and identify and then discuss the recommendations to reduce the risk of rollover injuries in 15-passenger vans.

Icy Road Conditions

A van full of students and luggage was traveling Interstate 70 in Colorado at approximately 45 miles per hour (72.4 km/h) on icy road conditions. The vehicle hit an icy spot causing the driver to lose control. The van spun a full 360 degrees on the pavement before coming to a stop in the median. No one was injured, but the potential for a disastrous wreck was enormous.

QUESTIONS

1. What is the appropriate reaction to the situation described in this scenario?

2. Winter driving conditions create increased hazards for drivers, especially those who may not be accustomed to driving in these conditions. What are some guidelines for winter driving?

3. What safety and season-specific equipment should be carried in vehicles during the winter? Explain why you chose each piece of equipment.

Trailer Towing Presents Risks

Two guides from the Great Falls Whitewater Adventure Program were scheduled to meet a group of 12 participants and their two teachers at Coal Banks Landing to start a 110-mile (177 km) river trip on Montana's Upper Missouri River. Unfortunately, they got off to a late start. Their plan was to drive a three-quarter-ton pickup truck loaded with paddling equipment, food, and camping gear and pulling a canoe trailer loaded with eight tandem canoes, and meet the group at the put-in. Once everything was loaded, the pair proceeded down the road. While en route, the pickup hit a large pothole, causing the trailer to bounce off the 2" ball hitch. It left the road, went down an embankment, and overturned. The trailer suffered some damage and was rendered unusable. Luckily, no boats were damaged.

QUESTIONS

1. What important item was missing that may have prevented the trailer from becoming completely detached from the pickup?

2. Are there other options for connecting a trailer to a vehicle that might be safer than the common ball and hitch?

3. As a program administrator, what practices could you implement to ensure safe trailer towing?

4. Create a checklist for inspecting boat and equipment trailers.

No Brakes

An instructor teaching a backpacking class at State College picked up her motor pool van for a fall weekend trip into a nearby national forest. The weekend went by quickly, and on Sunday morning the group reached the van. The group loaded the van, got settled in, and began the three-hour drive back to campus. The route back to campus included descending several miles on a winding, steep state highway to the interstate.

Approximately 30 minutes into the trip, the driver began the descent to the interstate. To maintain control around a curve, the driver applied the brakes and found that they did not work. She remained calm and took control of the situation by placing the vehicle into low gear and slowly engaging the emergency brake. This maneuver worked. As the vehicle slowed down, she was able to pull over onto the shoulder of the highway out of harm's way. After assessing the situation, the driver and the entire group walked approximately 1 mile (1.6 km) down the road to a private campground where she was able to call a tow truck.

The vehicle was towed into the nearest town, and the brakes were repaired. According to the mechanic who worked on the vehicle, the front brake pads were worn completely through and should have been replaced months ago. Three hours later the group was back on the road heading back to campus.

QUESTIONS

1. Many college and university programs use vehicles provided through their motor pools. As an adventure program provider, what are some steps you can take to make sure the vehicle you've picked up at the motor pool is in good repair?

2. Create a vehicle inspection checklist. Use this checklist to inspect the next vehicle you check out from the motor pool.

3. What safety equipment should be carried in program vehicles?

4. What are some practices your program undertakes to reduce transportation risks? Use the Haddon matrix to answer this question.

Glossary

accident—An unplanned, potentially dangerous occurrence that results in injury, property damage, or a near miss (Leemon et al., 1998).

accident potential—The possibility of an accident occurring.

assumption of risk—An agreement with a participant wherein the participant acknowledges awareness of certain risks inherent in the activity.

causation—Something that was done that results in an injury.

contract—An agreement between two or more parties in which an offer is made and accepted, and each party benefits.

due diligence—Precautions that a person or organization should take in light of the circumstances.

duty of care—An obligation to act toward others and the public with the degree of watchfulness, attention, caution, and prudence that a reasonable person in similar circumstances would have.

duty to warn—An obligation to warn others of a hazard.

emergency—Any serious incident or situation concerning health, injury, death, a missing person, or extensive property damage involving program participants, staff, guests, or property.

emergency action plan—A set of procedures designed to direct an organization's response to an accident.

foreseeability—The ability to know in advance that harm or injury may result from a negligent act.

guideline(s)—A suggested method of accomplishing a program activity, consistent with approved policy, that staff members should consider using, although they may adopt alternatives.

hazard—An unsafe condition or activity that, if left uncontrolled, can contribute to an accident.

incident—An event that occurs as a consequence of participating in an adventure or guided program that involves either the inherent risks of participating in an adventure activity, an accidental or intentional act, or involves an objective or subjective hazard.

industry standard—Established rules and generally accepted operating procedures, practices, and requirements defined by national associations and leading outdoor organizations in the adventure industry.

inherent risks—Risks that cannot be eliminated without changing the nature of the activity.

incident countermeasure—An action or actions taken in response to an injury or event to prevent it from recurring.

misadventure—An unlucky event or misfortune.

near miss—A close call, or "a dangerous situation where safety was compromised but did not result in injury" (Leemon & Schimelpfenig, 2003, pg. 178). An incident that did not result in injury, illness, or damage, but had the potential to do so.

negligence—The failure to use ordinary care: failing to do what a person of ordinary prudence would have done under the same or similar circumstances.

objective, or environmental, factors—Hazards that are usually quantifiable and represent the overall condition of the environment; also known as acts of God. Examples include weather, water conditions, and wildlife.

policy—Binding, overarching safety directives designed to influence and determine safety-related decisions.

procedure(s)—A specific instruction for accomplishing a program activity that staff members are required to follow except in exceptional circumstances.

proximate cause—Something that occurs which results in an injury due to negligence or an intentional wrongful act.

risk—A term applied to the individual or combined assessments of probability of loss and potential amount of loss.

risk avoidance—When the frequency and severity of risk are both high, program providers and guide services should consider canceling the program or activity.

risk control—Methods to reduce the amount of risk inherent in an activity.

risk evaluation—An element of risk management in which decisions are made about the importance and acceptability of risk.

risk factor—Something that increases the chances of a negative event occurring.

risk management—The systematic application of management policies, standards, and procedures to identify, analyze, assess, treat, and monitor risk.

risk reduction—When the severity of a potential risk remains low, but the overall frequency increases, organizations need to consider methods for reducing their exposure.

risk retention—The risk is identified and a decision is made to retain it and pay for any losses the organization may incur from the organization's own resources.

risk transfer—As the severity of risk potential increases, organizations transfer it to others. Transferring risk is the best option when the frequency of risk potential is low, but the severity of a potential incident is high.

safety—The U.S. National Safety Council defines safety as "the control of recognized hazards to attain an acceptable level of risk."

standard(s)—The level of conduct stipulated by associations of professionals in a region. Organizations or program staff operating below the standard may be held liable if a client is injured because of the low standard.

standard of care—The degree of attentiveness, caution, and prudence that a reasonable person in the same circumstances would exercise.

subjective hazard—Hazards that originate from the person and his or her inadequacies, such as overestimation of skills, knowledge, or the underestimation of difficulties.

tort—A civil wrong.

References

Adekoya, N., & Nolte, K.B. (2005). Struck-by-lightning: Deaths in the United States. *Journal of Environmental Health, 67* (9), 45-50.

American Institute for Avalanche Research and Education. (2011a). *Avalanche training courses*. Retrieved from http://avtraining.org/Avalanche-Training-Courses/Program-Overview.html.

American Institute for Avalanche Research and Education. (2011b). *US avalanche fatalities*. Retrieved from http://avtraining.org/.

Association for Experiential Education. (2009). *Manual of accreditation standards for adventure programs* (5th ed.). Boulder, CO: Association for Experiential Education.

Blanchard, J., Strong, M., & Ford, P. (2007). *Leadership and administration of outdoor pursuits* (3rd ed.). State College, PA: Venture Publishing.

Cloutier, R., & Valade, G. (n.d.). *Risk management for outdoor programs: A Handbook for administrators and instructors in British Columbia*. Victoria, BC: Center for Curriculum Transfer and Technology.

Colorado Avalanche Information Center. (2011). *US avalanche fatalities*. Retrieved from http://avalanche.state.co.us/acc/accidents_us.php.

Cooper, S., Buykx, P., McConnell-Henry, T., Kinsman, L., & McDermott, S. (2011). Simulation: Can it eliminate failure to rescue? *Nursing Times* 107, 3.

Cuskelly, G., & Auld, C.J. (1989). Retain, reduce, transfer or avoid? Risk management in sport organisations. *The ACHPER National Journal 23,* 17-20.

Ewert, A., & Shultis, J. (1999). Technology and backcountry recreation: Boon to recreation or bust for management? *Journal of Physical Education, Recreation & Dance 70* (8), 23-28.

Garner, B.A. (2009). *Black's law dictionary*. Egan, MN: West Publishing.

Haddad, K. (2010). *Outdoor Medical Incident Database (OMID)*. Retrieved from www.outward-bound.org/docs/safety/OMID.htm.

Haddon, W. (1972). A logical framework for categorizing highway safety phenomena and activity. *Journal of Trauma 12,* 1.

Hale, A. (1983). *Safety management for outdoor program leaders*. Unpublished manuscript.

Hansen-Stamp, C., & Gregg, R.G. (2002). Gearing up or down. *Outdoor Education and Recreation Law Quarterly 2* (2), 4, 19-20.

Heinrich, H.W. (1936). *Industrial accident prevention*. New York: McGraw-Hill.

Leemon, D. & Schimelpfenig, T. (2003). Wilderness Injury, Illness, and Evacuation: National Outdoor Leadership School's Incident Profiles, 1999–2002. *Wilderness and Environmental Medicine, 14*(3), 174-182.

Leemon, D., Schimelpfenig, T., Gray, S., Tarter, S, & Williamson, J. (1998). *Adventure program risk management report: 1998 Edition. Narratives and data from 1991-1997.* Boulder, CO: Association for Experiential Education.

Legal Dictionary. (2011). *Foreseeability.* Retrieved from http://legal-dictionary.thefree-dictionary.com/foreseeability.

Meyer, D. (1978). *Accident control and reporting responsibilities.* Unpublished manuscript, North Carolina Outward Bound School.

Moran, S., Box, B., Clark, S., Glenn, L., Kunz, L., & Wood, M.A. (2001). *Rocky terrain: A look at the risks in the outdoor adventure industry.* St. Paul, MN: The St. Paul Companies.

National Highway Traffic Safety Administration. (2008). *Traffic safety facts research notes: Fatalities to occupants of 15-passenger vans 1997-2006.* Retrieved from www-nrd.nhtsa.dot.gov/pubs/810947.pdf.

Niccolazzo, P. (2010). *The components of an effective staff development system.* Retrieved from www.outdoored.com/Articles/Article.aspx?ArticleID=203.

North Carolina Outward Bound. (2010). *Policy for field communication devices.* Unpublished manuscript.

Paulcke, W., & Dumler, H. (1976). *Hazards in mountaineering and how to avoid them.* New York: Oxford University Press.

Peanut Allergy. (2010). *Food Allergy Initiative.* Retrieved from www.faiusa.org.

Petzl Equipment. (2010). *Personal protection equipment inspection.* Retrieved from www.petzl.com/us/ppe-checking.

Sagan, S.D. (1995). *The limits of safety: Organizations, accidents, and nuclear weapons.* Princeton, NJ: Princeton University Press.

Steidl, R.J., & Powell, B.F. (2006). Assessing the effects of human activities on wildlife. *The George Wright Forum 23* (2), 50-58.

Snakes of North Carolina, (2011). *Timber rattlesnake.* Retrieved from www.herpsofnc.org/herps_of_nc/snakes/Crohor/Cro_hor.html

Turner, C.T. (2002). *Stopping rollovers: The dual-wheel solution for 15-passenger vans.* Washington, DC: The Public Citizen.

van der Smissen, B. (1990). *Legal liability and risk management for public and private entities.* Cincinnati, OH: Anderson.

Wade, I., & Fischesser, M. (1988). *A guide to conducting safety reviews for assessing and upgrading safety in outdoor adventure programs.* Unpublished manuscript.

About the Author

Aram Attarian, PhD, is an associate professor in the department of parks, recreation, and tourism management at North Carolina State University in Raleigh. He is the owner of the risk management consultation firm Adventureprogrammanagement.com and serves as the director of the National State Park Leadership School.

Attarian has over 30 years of experience in adventure education and outdoor leadership working with a range of individuals and settings, including adjudicated youth, college and university programs, businesses, camps, and Outward Bound. His most significant experiences have been with North Carolina Outward Bound (NCOB), where he worked as an instructor, climber, and course director for over 25 years.

Currently, Attarian serves on the NCOB board of directors and chairs its safety committee. He is also a member of the American Alpine Club Safety Advisory Council and is a regional contributor to *Accidents in North American Mountaineering.*

In his free time, Attarian enjoys rock climbing, outdoor living, and working on his hobby farm in western North Carolina. He resides in Raleigh.

You'll find other outstanding
recreation resources at
www.HumanKinetics.com

In the U.S. call 1.800.747.4457
Australia 08 8372 0999
Canada. 1.800.465.7301
Europe . . . . .+44 (0) 113 255 5665
New Zealand 0800 222 062

 HUMAN KINETICS
The Information Leader in Physical Activity & Health
P.O. Box 5076 • Champaign, IL 61825-5076